LEGAL ISSUES JOURNAL
Volume 8, Issue 2
July 2020

AF687654

Legal Issues Journal (LIJ) is a not-for-profit peer reviewed inter-disciplinary journal publishing original research in law, as well as inter-disciplinary research at the intersection of law and other disciplines, including genetics, biosciences, philosophy, linguistics, neuroscience, medicine and ethics. The core aim of the LIJ is to disseminate knowledge that contributes towards achieving justice – free from commercial considerations. The Journal publishes original papers, case comments, short reports, debates and book reviews. The Journal also provides interpretation articles on changes in the legal world and coming trends affecting law, lawyers, and society.

ISSN 2516-1210 (Print)
ISSN 2515-9887 (Online)

LEGAL ISSUES JOURNAL 8(2)

ISSN 2516-1210 (Print)
ISSN 2515-9887 (Online)

A Publication of the UKLSA
www.uklsa.co.uk

UKLSA

SULIS ACADEMIC PRESS
Published by Sulis Academic Press
An Imprint of Sulis International
Los Angeles | London
www.sulisinternational.com

The United Kingdom Law and Society Association (UKLSA)

www.uklsa.co.uk

Table of Contents

The Origin and Evaluation of Ship Breaking Regime of South Asia: A Critical Perspective From Bangladesh

Ishtiaque Ahmed[1]

Chair, Department of Law, North South University Bangladesh

Abstract: The Hong Kong Convention was adopted in 2009 to regulate the global industry of ship recycling, but the convention remains unenforced due to the problem of ratification by the leading ship recycling states. Due to the lopsided track record of shipbreaking in the last forty years, the ratification currently depends primarily on the policy choices of few developing nations. Given the gross unpreparedness and oversight of Pakistan towards the treaty's timely accession with India's recent ratification, and the ban of China on the import of hazardous waste, the responsibility lies with the policymakers of Bangladesh to decide the fate of this influential global pact. This article attempts to track down the origin and evolution of ship recycling regime of Bangladesh, followed by a critical analysis of the salient provisions of the framework ship recycling regulations of this chief ship recycling state as adopted recently. It postulates that the drawbacks figured out may create significant obstruction or procrastination to accede to the convention by Bangladesh thereby endowing an inclusive and sustainable global ship recycling industry any time soon. The article ends with recommendations to the government of Bangladesh for necessary amendments in its framework regulations on ship recycling identified in this research.

Keywords: Ship-breaking, Ship Recycling, Hong Kong Convention, End of Life Ships, Ship Breaking and Ship Recycling Rule.

---

[1]Corresponding author: ishtiaque.ahmed@northsouth.edu.

I. Introduction

A ship is the largest human-made moving object on the planet.[2] About 90% of world trade is carried by international shipping industry.[3] Ship-breaking or ship recycling, although is not a part of maritime navigation, is an essential part of maritime industry.[4] Ship recycling is a process of dismantling End of Life (EOL) vessels after their useful lives are over.[5] After about 25-30 years of continuous service, a ship becomes unseaworthy[6], dangerous for navigation & life at sea. When a ship's maintenance cost outweighs its income, the vessel outlives its utility;[7] it is then sent for scrapping as a matter of practical necessity. Around the world, annually, almost 1800 sea-going ships over 500 GT[8] become obsolete.[9] Several other modes of disposal of EOL ships are available globally but ship recycling remains the most sensible option, and currently

[2]*World's biggest Ship - (458 Metre long) largest human-made moving object in the world,* [Online Video], 2015, www.dailymotion.com/video/x2zchjg> (Accessed 19 March 2018).

[3]www.ics-shipping.org/shipping-facts/

[4]World Maritime Day message of IMO Secretary-General, Koji Sekimizu. See
United Nations Regional Information Centre for Western Europe (UNRIC), 2013
www.unric.org/en/latest-un-buzz/28709-sustainable-development-imos-contribution-beyond-rio20> (accessed 4 March 2017).

[5]Ishtiaque Ahmed, *Unravelling Socio-economic and Ecological Distribution Conflicts in Ship Breaking in Bangladesh for Addressing Negative Externalities in Law and Policy Making,* Minn. J. Int'l L. (2020) (forthcoming).

[6]*Id.*

[7]Tony George Puthucherril, *From Ship Breaking to Sutainable Ship Recycling Evolution of A Legal Regime 10* (Nijhoff Publishers, Netherlands, Martinus, 2010) (ebook).

[8]Gross tonnage (GT) is a nonlinear measure of a ship's overall internal volume.

[9]K. P. Jain, J. F. J. Pruyn, & J. J. Hopman, *Critical Analysis of the Hong Kong International Convention on Ship Recycling,* 7 International Journal of Environmental, Chemical, Ecological, Geological and Geophysical Engineering no. 10 684 (2013). Cited in N. Mikelis, *Hong Kong Convention: The origins of a convention,* (2012) (Presentation at World Maritime University, Malmo, Sweden).

there is no other feasible alternative.[10] Ship-breaking is considered as the most dangerous occupation in the world and is known as a pollution heavy industry.[11] The heaviness of environmental pollution and the casualties involved in ship-breaking are hardly comparable with other hazardous industries known in current time.[12]Sound management in ship breaking with optimum regard to the safety of life and environment raises critical question of economic viability of this very industrial activity.[13]

---

10 Matt Cohen, *Ship breaking Exports: Balancing Safe Disposal with Economic Realities*, 28 Envtl L. and Policy J. no. 2 245 (2005), www.environs.law.ucdavis.edu/volumes/28/2/cohen.pdf (last visited Jan. 4, 2018). Cited in Jeffrey Luster, *The Domestic and International Legal Implications of Exporting Hazardous Waste: Exporting Naval Vessels for Scrapping*, 7 Envtl L. 85 (2001).

11 Ishtiaque Ahmed, *Safe & Environmentally Sound Recycling of Ships: A Stocktaking of the Current State of International Law*, 31 Fordham Envtl. L. Rev. 60 (2020).

12 Interview with Md. Ali Shahin, Coordinator, YPSA and Bangladesh Representative of NGO Ship Breaking platform, Chittagong (Aug. 5, 2016) [hereinafter Ali Shahin Interview].

13 A US ship breaking yard in 2011 confirmed the cost of ship breaking as follows: War ship USD 900 to 1300 per LDT, Military vessel USD 300 to 700 per LDT and commercial vessel USD 100 to 500 per LDT. *See* Gopal Krishna Chowdhary, *An analysis of the creation of a global ship recycling fund in the framework of the Hong Kong International Convention for the Safe and Environmentally Sound Recycling of Ships, 2009*, World Maritime University 54 (2011), www.commons.wmu.se/cgi/viewcontent.cgi?referer= www.bing.com/ &httpsredir=1&article=1101&context=all_dissertations (last visited Mar. 12, 2018) (MSc Thesis). According to the recent market, in 2017-2018, ships are sold by cash buyers in South Asian ship breaking yards at the rate on average USD 300 per LDT. *See* Xiaolin Zeng, *Ship scrap prices up on higher steel prices*, Fair Play (Feb. 21, 2017), www.fairplay.ihs.com/commerce/article/4282391/ship-scrap-prices-up-on-higher-steel-prices (last visited Jan. 4, 2018).

II. Ship Breaking Industry and South Asia

The international industry of ship breaking was a highly mechanized industry until it piled up in South Asian beaches in 1980s.[14] Beginning from the mid-1980s, the southern region and peninsula of Asia has turned into the global epicenter of ocean-going ship recycling.[15] Over 80 percent of obsolete vessels from around the world, since the 1980s, have been sent only to three countries of South Asia namely Bangladesh, India and Pakistan.[16] The availability of cheap labor,[17] geographical advantage, favorable weather conditions, and huge demand of scrap metals in the growing construction industries, as well as lack of enforcement of workers' rights, environmental and coastal laws are believed to be the predominant reasons for its progressive transition to these nations of poorer economy.[18]

Bangladesh, a newly developing country,[19] has emerged as the market leader in ocean going ship recycling, transforming the highest amount of

---

[14]Muhammad Muhibbullah, 'Health hazards and risks vulnerability of ship breaking workers: A case study on Sitakunda ship breaking industrial area of Bangladesh', *Global Advanced Research Journal of Geography and Regional Planning*, vol.2, no.8, p. 173, Available from: www.shipbreakingplatform.org/shipbrea_wp2011/wp-content/uploads/2014/12/Health-hazards-and-risks-vulnerability-of-ship-breaking-works-Muhibbullah-Nov-2013.pdf (accessed 4 July 2017)

[15]Sohanur Rahman, *Aspects and Impacts of Ship Recycling in Bangladesh,* 194 Procedia Engineering 271 (2017), ScienceDirect (10th International Conference on Marine Technology, Dhaka, 2016).

[16]Nicola Mulinaris , *The toxic trade of obsolete ships*, The Ecologist (Oct. 15, 2018), https://theecologist.org/2018/oct/15/toxic-trade-obsolete-ships.

[17]*Id.*

[18]In 1960 UK and USA was the market leader in ship recycling. *See* Bright Hub Engineering (2016), www.brighthubengineering.com/marine-engines-machinery/63667-marine-engineering-scrapping-and-recycling-ships/ (last visited Feb. 4, 2018).

[19]Bangladesh, a Least Developed Country (LDC), recently has fulfilled the eligibility criteria of the United Nations to be recognized as a developing country. Bangladesh will now be eligible able to apply to the UN to be recognized as a developing country. It is expected that formal transition will take place by 2024. *See* Sairas Rahman, *Bangladesh on path to be recognized as a developing country*, Dhaka Tribune (Mar. 17, 2018), www.dhakatribune.com/bangladesh/2018/03/17/bangladesh-path-recognized-developing-country/.

recyclable tonnage from EOL vessels, both in LDT measurement[20] and in terms of number of ships dismantled annually.[21] In 2019, Bangladesh met almost half of the global demand for decommissioning obsolete vessels.[22] Notably, the predominant ship dismantling practice that occurs in Bangladesh and its neighbouring competitors, India and Pakistan, is known as 'beach breaking' or 'beaching'.[23]

Beaching is considered the most treacherous, but the least expensive, method of recycling currently available worldwide.[24] In this method, ships are run full steam ahead during high tide towards the sea shore until the vessel is finally grounded on the mud flat on the beach. The ship is then gradually winched forward up the beach, bit by bit in semidiurnal tidal water.[25] Workers get on board the ship to begin dismantling operations using mainly traditional tools and techniques. Ship breaking on the beach of the Southern peninsula of Asia is a controversial activity,[26] where human casualty and irreversible degradation of marine environment have been an alarming phenomenon. Almost 700 lives have been lost and 10,000 workers have suffered from permanent disability only in Bangladesh in last three decades.[27] In South Asia, the average rate of accident and death in the beach breaking sites have remained unchanged

---

[20]Syed Mansur Hashim, *A graveyard for ships and men*, The Daily Star (Oct. 24, 2017),
www.thedailystar.net/opinion/no-frills/graveyard-ships-and-men-1480753.

[21]Anwar Hussain, *Bangladesh secures top position in ship breaking*, Dhaka Tribune (Nov. 14, 2019),
www.dhakatribune.com/bangladesh/2019/11/14/bangladesh-secures-top-position-in-ship-breaking
(last visited Apr. 20, 2020).

[22]*Id.*

[23]Henrik Hagberg Partner, *Scrapping of Ships, is Beaching Illegal?* Thommessen (Nov. 14, 2018),
www.thommessen.no/en/news/scrapping-of-ships-is-beaching-illegal (last visited Apr. 20, 2020).

[24]*Id.*

[25]Ishtiaque Ahmed, Unravelling Socio-Economic and Ecological Distribution Conflicts in Shipbreaking in Bangladesh for Addressing Negative Externalities in Law and Policy Making, 29 Minn. J. Int'l L. 161 (2020)

[26]Elin Saltkjel, Head of QA and Business Development, Grieg Green AS and Kan Matsuzaki, Director, Industry All Union, Interviewed by Author, 2020, ACI Ship Recycling Congress 2020, Amsterdam, The Netherlands

[27]Saiful Karim, *Violation of labour rights in the ship-breaking yards of Bangladesh: legal norms and reality*, 25 Int'L J. of Comparative Labor Law and Industrial Relations no. 4 380 (2009),
HeinOnline (last visited July 5, 2016).

since last several decades.[28] According to United Nation Environment Program (UNEP), shipbreaking activities remain the largest land source marine pollution in South Asia[29]. Unilateral regulations to control the industry have been ineffective, given the industry's global character with the large number of actors involved internationally.[30] According to many, there has been an urgent necessity to forge a global regime to jointly control all aspects of the industry.[31]

III. Regulating Global Ship Breaking Industry

After three decades of anarchy and lawlessness in global ship recycling activity , the Hong Kong Convention for the Safe and Environmentally Sound Recycling of Ship 2009 shortly, the Hong Kong Convention (HKC) was adopted under the auspicious International Maritime organization (IMO) [32] but the convention has failed to see the light of success because of the difficulty in fulfilling its three stage entry into force criteria.

---

[28]*Ship Breaking-Recycling, Old Cruise Ships*, Cruisemapper 9, www.cruisemapper.com/wiki/768-ship-breaking (last visited Apr. 20, 2020).

[29]Ljubomir Jeftic, Seba Sheavly, & Ellik Adler, *Marine Litter: A Global Challenge*, UNEP 148 (2009), www.wedocs.unep.org/bitstream/handle/20.500.11822/7787/-Marine%20Litter_%20A%20Global%20Challenge%20%282009%29-2009845.pdf?sequence=3&isAllowed=y (last visited Mar. 15, 2018).

[30]Valentina Rossi, *The Dismantling of End of Life Ships: The Hong Kong Convention for the safe and environmentally sound recycling of ships*, Italian Yearbook of Int'l L. 278 (2011), www.sidi-isil.org/wp-content/uploads/2010/12/Yearbook2011_rossi.pdf (last visited Feb. 4, 2017).

[31]Puthucherril, *supra* note 3, at 52.

[32]IMO (2018), www.imo.org/en/OurWork/Environment/ShipRecycling/Pages/Default.aspx (last visited Jan. 4, 2018). The International Maritime Organization is a specialised agency of the United Nations responsible for regulating shipping. See www.imo.org/en/About/Pages/Default.aspx

As per the entry into force criteria of this global treaty, ratification by both ship owning and ship recycling states[33] having certain track record of history of ship recycling ten years preceeding the date of accession is essential.[34] For the last several decades, the industrially developed countries which mostly belong to the ship owning nations were hardly associated with EOL ship recycling.[35] Most leading ship recycling states, representing the developing nations, have negligible number of merchant fleets registered in their registries.[36] Due to this lopsided track record in the history of shipbreaking, the success of this convention now depends primarily on the policy choices of these South Asian ship recycling nations.[37] The position does not change even if the whole world ratifies the convention, including China, the fourth largest ship recycling state in the

[33]The top ten ship owning nations currently, in terms of hierarchy, belongs to Japan, Greece, China , Singapore, Norway, South Korea , USA, Germany, UK and Denmark see https://safety4sea.com/top-10-shipowning-nations/ On the other hand four main ship recycling countries (Bangladesh, India, Pakistan and Turkey) currently recycling almost 96 percent of all tonnage with China and rest of the world's share is simply nugatory. See www.maritime-executive.com/editorials/developments-in-ship-recycling-in-2019

[34]HKC Art. 17

[35]*Ship Dismantling and Pre-cleaning of Ships*, European Commission Directorate General Environment 23 (June 2007), www.ec.europa.eu/environment/waste/ships/pdf/ship_dismantling_report.pdf (last visited Jan. 4, 2018).

[36]UNCTAD, Merchant Fleet by Country of Beneficial Ownership, annual https://unctadstat.unctad.org/wds/TableViewer/tableView.aspx?ReportId=80100

[37]*Two Roads for Hong Kong Convention to Enter into Force*, The Maritime Executive, (Mar. 31, 2019), (last visited May. 14, 2020). www.maritime-executive.com/editorials/two-roads-for-hong-kong-convention-to-enter-into-force>

world.[38] In other words, the ratification by the whole world has little meaning to this convention unless any two of these four giant ship recycling states, namely Bangladesh, India, Pakistan and China accede to the convention.[39] However after India's recent accession to the HKC in December 2019, the fate of the convention is now clearly depends on the policy choices of one of the remaining three leading ship recycling states.

However, a closer look reveals that pursuant to the legal and recent political position of China, the ratification of the convention is extremely unlikely, given the recent ban on importing foreign EOL ships for recycling in China[40] By taking this move, China to a great extent has denied the transcontinental character of this convention. As per the HKC, a member state is also not allowed to discriminate between party and non-party ships in their treatment on recycling of ships.[41] Predictably on ratification of the convention, how China would address the issue of discrimination between party states remains questionable.[42] Furthermore, China belongs to the top five ship owning states.[43] The ratification by

---

[38]In last three decades five countries of the world have recycled 98% ships worldwide. The recycling capacities of China plus Turkey plus the rest of the world (but excluding the three South Asian countries) does not fulfill the third entry into force condition. On the other hand, the combined capacities of China plus any one out of the three South Asian ship recycling countries meet the requirement of the third condition see *India Prepares to Ratify the Hong Kong Convention*, The Maritime Executive (Dec. 2, 2017), www. maritime-executive.com/article/india-prepares-to-ratify-the-hong-kong-convention#gs.rdVU5cI (last visited May. 14, 2020). For ship recycling record in last four decades See www.imo.org/en/KnowledgeCentre/PapersAndArticlesByIMOStaff/Documents/SHIPREC%202013%20-%20International%20Conference%20on%20Ship%20Recycling.pdf , (last visited May 14, 2020).

[39]*Id.*

[40]*China bans scrapping of foreign ships at its yards*, Safety4Sea (May 8, 2018), www. safety4sea.com/china-bans-scrapping-of-foreign-ships-at-its-yards/ (last visited Mar. 4, 2018).

[41]HKC art. 3.4.

[42]Ishtiaque Ahmed, *Safe & Environmentally Sound Recycling of Ships: A Stocktaking of the Current State of International Law*, 31 Fordham Envtl. L. Rev. 65 (2020).

[43]*UNCTAD reveals top 5 ship-owning countries*, Safety4Sea (Nov. 3, 2017), https://safety4sea.com/unctad-reveals-top-5-ship-owning-countries 2utm_sourcesafety4seautm_mediummajors/ (last visited Mar. 4, 2018).

China will likely add another 8.8 percent of the world's fleet.[44] This would satisfy the second entry into force criteria of the HKC[45] but make the fulfillment of the third entry condition more onerous than what it exists currently.[46] For the same reason, Liberia and Marshall Islands, the second and third largest ship owning states[47] have already been advised by the IMO not to accede to the HKC unless China, Bangladesh or Pakistan ratifies the convention first.[48] Given the latest position of China, it is extremely unlikely for this state to accede to the convention any time soon.

It is noted that non-ratification by China seems hardly influence the global business of ship recycling. Shipping owners in China receive a significant subsidy from their government for choosing their ships to be recycled in China.[49] Almost all Chinese ships are now being recycled in China only, as a result.[50] China belongs to one of the largest shipping nations in the world and as per the report of UNCTAD, the Republic of Korea, Japan and China built 91.8% of world gross tonnage in the year

---

[44]Dr. Nikos Mikelis, *Two Roads for Hong Kong Convention to Enter into Force*, The Maritime Executive 9 (Mar. 31, 2019), www.maritime-executive.com/editorials/two-roads-for-hong-kong-convention-to-enter-into-force (last visited Mar. 11, 2020).

[45]*Id.*

[46]*Id.* at 7.

[47]*Top 10 flag states 2019*, Lloyd's List (Dec. 3, 2019), www.lloydslist.maritimeintelligence.informa.com/LL1129840/Top-10-flag-states-2019 (last visited Mar. 11, 2020).

[48]Mikelis, *supra* note 31, at 11.

[49]E Grey, 'Is China's shipbreaking industry close to breaking point?', *Ship Technology,*1 November 2016, *para.* Government subsidies see the industry through tough times, **a**vailable from: www.ship-technology.com/features/featureis-chinas-shipbreaking-industry-close-to-breaking-point-5654499/ (accessed 4 March 2018)

[50]According to Dr. Mikelis, Former head of ship recycling division at IMO, and currently the non-executive director of GMS cash buyer, a significant amount of subsidy is paid to a Chinese shipowner who recycles a Chinese flagged ship in a Chinese recycling yard. The level of the subsidy has reached to an astounding figure which is around $400 to $440 per LDT. This amount is more than the best price paid by yard owners in Bangladesh, India, or Pakistan. Moreover, on top of this subsidy, the shipowners are also paid a sum of around $200 per LDT from the yard. According to Mikelis, these incidents have made the Chinese ship owners crazy to recycling their ship only in China see W Laursen, 'Chinese Subsidies Spark Shipbreaking Debate,' *The Maritime Executive*, 12 April 2015, Available from, https://maritime-executive.com/article/chinese-subsidies-spark-shipbreaking-debate#gs.ZVkmHNM >(accessed 4 March 2018).

2016.[51] China owns the largest share of the General Cargo Vessels in the world.[52] China being the owners of 11% of global tonnage[53] recycles about 10% of the world tonnages.[54] It's not therefore a surprise to learn that bulk of the tonnages recycled in China are owned by Chinese owners only and this country is not in direct competition with South Asia. Besides, in domestic law, beaching is declared illegal in China.[55]

On the other hand, except being a domestic instrument dealing with allocation of plots for ship recycling yards, provisions on tariff and custom duties, and allocation of ship recycling plots by the government, Pakistan has a rudimentary legal mechanism that is specifically designed to deal with the safety, health and environment in ship-breaking.[56] The industry relies solely on general laws applicable to any other ordinary heavy industries.[57] Therefore it is also very unlikely for Pakistan to utilize these un-mellowed legal instruments to accede to the HKC any time soon.[58]

---

[51]'UNCTAD reveals top 5 ship-owning countries', Safety4Sea, 3 November 2017, Available from:
https://safety4sea.com/unctad-reveals-top-5-ship-owning-countries 2utm_sourcesafety4seautm_mediummajors/> (accessed 4 March 2018).
[52]*Ibid*
[53]International Shipping News, 'China-owned ships: fleet expansion accelerates,' Hellenic Shipping News, *15 March 2016*, Available from www.hellenicshippingnews.com/china-owned-ships-fleet-expansion-accelerates/> (accessed 4 March 2018).
[54]NGO Shipbreaking platform, '2016 List of all ships scrapped worldwide -Facts and Figures, Brussels, 2017,
Available from: www.shipbreakingplatform.org/shipbrea_wp2011/wp-content/uploads/2017/02/Stats-Graphs_2016-List_FINAL1.pdf >(accessed 4 March 2018).
[55]Xie D, 'Present situation and future development of the ship recycling industry in China, Hong Kong', 2007, www.bimco.org/sitecore/shell/ Control> cited in K Sivaprasad, 'Development of best practices for ship recycling processes', Ph.D. thesis, Cochin University of Science and Technology, 2010, Chapter -2, p. 13.
www.shodhganga.inflibnet.ac.in/bitstream/ 10603/3139/12/12_chapter%202.pdf
[56]Kanwar Muhammad Javed Iqbal, & Patrizia Heidegger, *Pakistan Shipbreaking Outlook: The Way Forward for a Green Ship Recycling Industry–Environmental, Health and Safety Conditions*, NGO Shipbreaking Platform 16 (2013),
www.shipbreakingplatform.org/wp-content/uploads/2019/01/SDPI-NSP-Pakistan-Position-Paper-For-Printing.pdf (last visited Mar. 11, 2020).
[57]*Id.*
[58]Ishtiaque Ahmed, *Safe & Environmentally Sound Recycling of Ships: A Stocktaking of the Current State of International Law*, 31 Fordham Envtl. L. Rev. 66 (2020).

According to the third entry into force criteria of the HKC, the combined maximum for annual ship recycling volume of the states, 10 years preceding to the date of ratification, must constitute not less than three percent of the combined merchant shipping tonnages of the same State.[59] After India's ratification of the convention in December 2019, the current figure reflects 2.6%.[60] Based on the historical records of ship recycling in the last 40 years globally, it is evident that the ball remains now in the court of Bangladesh, who retains the key to the enforcement leading towards the success of this treaty.[61] It should be mentioned here that the scope of this article is not to go into the details of the provisions of the HKC but to attempt, from a doctrinal perspective, to focus on the evaluation and critical analysis of the framework regulations on ship recycling of Bangladesh. Bangladesh is currently the largest and the most dominent ship recycling state currenty in the world. Attempt will be made to evaluate, in general, the state's appositeness to acceed to the global treaty on ship recycling at its current predicament of legislations.

Iv. Ship Breaking in Bangladesh

Traditionally the largest section of the global shipping industry counts on Bangladesh for disposal of their obsolete vessels from international waters.[62] Bangladesh recently has designed its domestic framework regulation on ship recycling taking note of the HKC.[63] These include Ship Breaking and Ship Recycling Rule 2011 (Hereinafter referred as the SBRR 2011) and Hazardous Waste and Ship Breaking Hazardous Waste

[59]HKC art. 17.
[60]*India Ratifies Hong Kong Convention*, IndustriALL 7 (2018), www.industriall-union.org/worlds-largest-shipbreaking-country-ratifies-hong-kong-convention
(last visited Mar. 11, 2020).
[61]Ishtiaque Ahmed, 'Hong Kong Convention and the Framework Legislations on Ship Recycling in Bangladesh: A Gap Analysis for the Purpose of the Effective Implementation of the Convention', (IMO Seminar on Ship Recycling and the Hong Kong Convention, Zhoushan, China, 23 -25 July 2019)
[62]Monira Munni, *Bangladesh Top Dumping Ground for Ships*, The Financial Express (Feb. 7, 2020), https://thefinancialexpress.com.bd/trade/bangladesh-top-dumping-ground-for-ships-1581051205 (last visited Apr. 20, 2020).
[63]*The Ship Breaking and Ship Recycling Rules, 2011*, (Dec. 12, 2011), https://moind.portal.gov.bd/sites/default/files/files/moind.portal.gov.bd/legislative_information/52017f63_a708_40d2_a95a_529a01e9bb7c/SBSBR2011.compressed%20(1).pdf
(Government circulation no. 36.061.016.07.00.021.2010-106).

Management Rule 2011 (Hereinafter referred as the HWR 2011). In 2018, Bangladesh adopted Ship Recycling Act (SRA 2018) that mostly deals with allocation of ship recycling zones, constitution and operation of the regulatory board named Bangladesh Ship Recycling Board (BSRB)[64] dedicated to administering the ship breaking industry in Bangladesh and a number of penal provisions.[65] Importantly the 2018 Act has created a statutory obligation for Bangladesh to develop legal and technical capacity to conform to the provisions of the HKC within five years of the date of commencement of this Act, in other words by February 2023.[66]

Arguably, the ship recycling framework regulations of this country appear to have attained a transnational character in the true sense of the term.[67] For the next decade or so, the legal and political position of Bangladesh may potentially decide the fate of this influential global pact. The domestic ship recycling legislations of Bangladesh guide most of the global shipping companies around the world as they prefer to recycle their ships in Bangladeshi yards. For better understanding of the topic, this article will attempt to plunge into a brief history and an evolution of the ship recycling regime of this crowing ship recycling state.

V. Evolution of Ship Recycling Regime in Bangladesh

Ship-breaking began in Bangladesh in much inorganized fashion. Two separate incidents are believed to the framer of confidence in business-men which ultimately gave birth to this country as the epicenter of global ship recycling industry.[68] In 1965 a Greek ship, *M.V Alpin* stranded in the Bay of Bengal, was successfully dismantled by the 'Chittagong Steel Mill'[69] with the help of local inhabitants and its workers using mostly traditional tools and techniques.[70] Subsequently a Pakistani ship, *"Al Abbas"* damaged by bombing during the liberation war in 1971, was salvaged on the beach of Chittagong, Bangladesh and successfully disman-

---

[64]Bangladesh Ship Recycling Act, 2018 § 4

[65]Bangladesh Ship Recycling Act, 2018 § 7.2.

[66]Bangladesh Ship Recycling Act, 2018 § Chapter VII.

[67]Transnational law includes law that regulates actions or events that transcend national frontiers includes domestic laws. *See* Chapter Ii A Basic Introduction to Transnational Law,
63, www.law.berkeley.edu/php-programs/courses/fileDL.php?fID=7587.

[68]Michael H. Gavshon, *The Ship Breakers*, Youtube (2013), www.youtube.com/watch?v=PdYK2vb6McE (last visited May. 13, 2020).

[69]*Id.*

[70]*Id.*

tled entirely manually in 1974 by the workers of 'Karnafully Metal Works.'[71]

Beginning in the early 1980s, the business of ship recycling in Bangladesh progressed smoothly and profitably, thanks to cheap labor and minimum infrastructure, despite pressure mounted steadily by the environmental, labor and human rights activists resisting progress of this questionable activity on the pristine beach of this relatively small country.[72] In 2008, the protestation culminated in the seminal case,"*MT Enterprise*", filed by Bangladesh Environmental Lawyers Association (BELA) in the Supreme Court of Bangladesh[73], against the Government's decision to allow the import of a tanker named '*MT Enterprise*' for dismantling.[74]

Since the beginning, the ship-breaking was steered by the Department of Shipping (DoS)[75] who had limited or no experience in labor management or environmental issues.[76] The Supreme Court unearthed measurable failure of the government to comply with rules on environmental clearances including directions made earlier by the Supreme Court to frame rules governing hazardous activities and industries in Bangladesh.[77] In 2009, the Court, acting *Suo moto*, issued nine specific directives upon the government, including instant closure of all ship breaking yards operating without clearance from the Department of Environment (DoE), which ultimately affected all the facilities, as none of them had been operating with valid environmental clearances.[78] Despite

---

[71]Khandakar Akhter Hossain, *Ship Recycling Practice and Annual Reusable Material Output from Bangladesh Ship Recycling Industry*, 7 J. Of Fundamentals of Renewable Energy and Applications no. 5 2 (2017), www.omicsonline.org/open-access/ship-recycling-practice-and-annual-reusable-material-output-from-bangladesh-ship-recycling-industry-2090-4541-1000238.php?aid=93707.

[72]Ship Breaking Bangladesh (2012), www.shipbreakingbd.info/shipbreaking%20in%20news.html.

[73]Bangladesh Supreme Court has two divisions, High Court Division and Appellate Division, of which the latter is the Apex Court of the country.

[74]It was a Public Interest Litigation (PIL) under art. 102 (2) (a) (i) and (ii) of the Constitution of the People's Republic of Bangladesh.
In the Writ Petition No. 7260 of 2008 Bangladesh Environmental Lawyers Association (BELA). 17 March 2009

[75]Interview with Captain K.M Jashim Uddin Sarker, Master Mariner (Class-1 UK), Chief Nautical Surveyor, Department of Shipping, Govt. of Bangladesh, Dhaka (July 25, 2016). Interview with Md. Alamgir Khan, Director, Department of Shipping, Govt. of Bangladesh, Dhaka (July 25, 2016).

[76]Writ Petition No. 7260 of 2008 *supra* note 57.

[77]*Id.* at 15.

[78]*Id.* at 18.

the year-long passing of judgment on 17 March 2009 by the highest court of the country, the government among other respondents failed to comply with any of the directives of the court, including the framing of rules.[79] The condition of the recycling yards remained unchanged.[80] Time petitions were filed by the government on several occasions on many insubstantial grounds.[81] More shockingly, ships were still being imported in clear violation of injunction against import, triggering several other contempt proceedings against violators and all of which remained pending.[82]

It is noted that Bangladesh is one of the poorest and most densely populated countries in the world. Poverty is widespread, affecting almost 50 percent of the population.[83] Eventually, the reality of this poor[84] labor surplus country [85] was addressed before the court. The emblematic social, economic, national, and international politics hindward the industry took precedence. The voice of the court subdued in a subsequent petition moved by the respondents. The government argued that no goal can be achieved overnight, and if the ban is not lifted immediately, an economic disaster is inevitable.[86] The petitioner was able to convince the court that not only members of the owners association were in financially impacted and otherwise, but also the masses had been affected because of the ban on the import of EOL ships.[87] They averred that the prohibition had placed tremendous pressure on the job market, causing significant reduction of supply of raw materials to specific industries and increased prices of many common and essential items.[88] The court disposed of the rule,

---

[79]*Id.* at 21.

[80]The court observed in its order dated Feb. 8, 2010 that approximately 350 other vessels have been imported and brought into Bangladesh for breaking and the number of authorized ship breaking facility increased from 36 to 68 in just 12 months. But the Government failed to provide precise information if they have been issued with any environmental clearance certificate as required by the HC in earlier directives. Meanwhile, in just one year, 24 persons have met their death at the shipbreaking yards with numerous permanent injuries.

[81]Interview with Advocate Rizwana Hasan, Chief Executive Officer, Bangladesh Environmental Lawyers Association, Dhaka, Bangladesh (Aug. 5, 2016).

[82]*Id.*

[83]p.246, www.fairlabor.org/sites/default/files/documents/reports/2004_annual_public_report_part4.pdf

[84]www.newagebd.net/article/57482/poverty-behind-much-of-child-labour

[85]https://bea-bd.org/site/images/pdf/010.pdf

[86]*Bangladesh Environmental Lawyers Association v. Government of Bangladesh,* Writ Petition (Civil) No. 7260/2008 (Order of the Supreme Court dated 7 March 2011)

[87]*Ibid*

[88]*Ibid*

lifting the ban on the import of EOL ships pending the adoption and enforcement of the rule subject to 18 revised and specific directions upon the ship recyclers and the government.[89] This decision effectively withdrew the previous requirement of decontamination of EOL ships before they are imported to Bangladesh territory. Importantly the later directive of the Supreme Court was a significant move from the rigor of the earlier one. According to this new directive except tankers, no ship is required to be certified gas free until driven onto the beach for recycling.[90] This action was adequately covered in the earlier directive number eight, where pre-cleaning of ships at the source was mandatory.[91] The pre-cleaning includes complete removal of oily waste from all ship's tank, bilge water tanks, lube oil tanks, engine room, ballast tanks , paints in the hull, and all other loose hazardous materials including the complete removal of all hazardous materials that remain as part of the ships inbuilt structure.[92] The Ministry of Environment and Forestry (MoEF) was directed for the second time to frame rules governing hazardous waste industry in Bangladesh in line with the Environment Conservation Act 1995, Factory Act 1965, Labor Act 2006, Basel Convention 1989, Hong Kong Convention 2009, Basel Technical guidelines and ILO guidelines of Ship Recycling within three months of the judgment being served upon them.[93] During the pendency of the suit, the Government declared ship breaking as a formal industry, amended the rules of business and the Ministry of Industry (MoI) was charged with entire responsibility for regulating shipbreaking in Bangladesh.[94]

Accordingly, on 14 December 2011, the government submitted before the Supreme Court, a tailor-made domestic regulation on ship recycling titled '*Ship Breaking & Recycling Rule 2011*' (SBRR 2011) after a gazette notification on 12 December 2011. This instrument was the first ever tailor-made framework regulation adopted by a country that relies solely on beaching method of recycling of ships. A further regulation titled '*Hazardous Waste and Ship Breaking Hazardous Waste Manage-*

---

[89]*Id. See also* Staff Reporter, *Court decision allowed the industry to restart the import of scrap vessels*, Safety4Sea (June 14, 2011), https://safety4sea.com/bangladesh-ship-breakers-back-in-business-after-the-easing-of-strict-environmen/#.

[90]Judgment of March 7, 2011 *supra* note 69.

[91]Judgment of March 17, 2009 *supra* note 57.

[92]Seminar on Ship Breaking and Ship Recycling in Bangladesh and Compliance with International Regulations Tuesday, 17 January 2012, BUET https://name.buet.ac.bd/ShipBreakingandRecyclingSeminar17012012.pdf

[93]*Id.* at 21.

[94]https://moind.gov.bd/site/page/9d79706a-cffd-4d70-9966-547b7697cc3d/Allocation-of-Business

ment Rule 2011' (Herein after referred to as the HWR 2011) was also adopted by the DoE under the power granted by the ECA 1995. This regulation implemented the Basel Convention in ship-breaking industry and other industries in Bangladesh dealing with hazardous wastes.[95] In 2018, *Ship Recycling Act* (SRA 2018) was adopted by the Ministry of Industry to provide additional legal basis for the framework legislations already adopted in pursuant to the order of the High Court and to allow the government to develop additional rules or amend the existing rules for the management , development, and advancement of the Ship- breaking Industry in Bangladesh.

Vi. The Shipbreaking and Recycling Rule 2011 (Sbrr 2011):

The Definition of Ship

In SBRR 2011, the term 'ship' has been very widely defined and includes

> Vessels and floating structures of any type operated in the marine environment and shall include submersibles, floating structures, floating platform, self-elevating platforms, floating storage unit, floating production storage unit and offloading units, a vessel stripped of equipment or being towed; destined for breaking purposes.[96]

The above suggests that the rule did not exclude even a small-scaled riverboat that may operate in an inland marine environment. The definition of 'ship' does not also prohibit inland water vessels, coastal ships, government ships or warships of any type, capacity or size.

Arrival of EOL Ships in Bangladesh:

The SBRR 2011 requires both the EOL ships and the ship recycling facility (SRF) owners separately to notify the competent authority (CA) about their intention to recycle a ship before its arrival at the state territory in due time. EOL ships are frequently arrested both at the point of exit from the exporting states or when entering the ship recycling states due to the application of UN Basel Convention worldwide or the European Waste

[95]HWR 2011 Rule 17.
[96]SBBR 2011. at § 2 (vii).

Shipment Regulation (EUSRR)[97] in EU ports.[98]Any arrest of an EOL ship at an anchorage of the recycling state or a stay order of the court either before or after it is taken to the facility leads to an obvious negative financial consequences for ship recyclers.[99] Ship recyclers mostly rely on bank loans with high rate of interest to import ships for breaking.[100] It costs in average BDT 175 crore (equivalent to 21 million USD) approximately to buy a scrap ship.[101] Generally, ship recyclers must pay bank interest at the rate of 15% to 16% per annum.[102] To an importer this creates an indebtedness to bank by BDT 4,000 per day per crore totaling seven lacs per day (equivalent to USD 8,300 approximately) only.[103]The financial stake for an unnecessary delay even for a single day is therefore exceedingly high. The overhead cost of a ship waiting at the anchorage for beaching is also considerable.[104] These matters prompt them to rush into action and complete the beaching and cutting formalities as quickly as possible. Pursuit of EOL ships proceeding to the recycling states, by the anti-beaching campaigners both at home and abroad has never been absent.[105] The more the recyclers, in the circumstances can delay this notification of arrival, the more they can reduce the chance of adverse media coverage to which they are regularly exposed. An unflagging tug of war between yard owners and green activists in all three South Asian shipbreaking nations is noticeable. An undercover operation therefore provides a practical benefit to the recyclers in the circumstance.

---

[97]EUSRR implemented Basel Convention in the EU

[98]Charles Digges, *Danish shipping giant caught beaching ships in India and Bangladesh,* Bellona (Oct. 20, 2016), www.bellona.org/news/industrial-pollution/2016-10-danish-shipping-giant-caught-beaching-ships-in-india-and-bangladesh. *Note* that The EU West Recycling Regulation is the implementing regulation of the Basel Convention.

[99]Interview with MA Hashem, Director, Mother Steel Limited, at Chittagong, Bangladesh (Aug. 10–15, 2016); Interview with Monjur Morshed, Owner, OWW Trading and Ship Breaking, at Chittagong, Bangladesh (Aug. 10–15, 2016).

[100]Ishtiaque Ahmed, *Unmasking the Critical Participants in Shipbreaking Industry for Apportioning Their Role in Law and Policy Making: A Perspective from Bangladesh,* Sturm College of Law Univ. Of Denver Transportation L. J. (2020) (forthcoming).

[101]Shohag Kumar Biswash, SA TV News at 10.30 pm (Apr. 3, 2020).

[102]Ahmed, *supra* note 82.

[103]Kumar Biswash, *supra* note 83.

[104]Ishtiaque Ahmed, *The Basel Convention on the Control of Transboundary Movements of Hazardous Wastes and Their Disposal: A Legal Misfit in Global Ship Recycling Jurisprudence,* 29 Wash. L. Rev. 411 (2020). https://digitalcommons.law.uw.edu/wilj/vol29/iss2/7/ at 423.

[105]*Id* at 424.

To avoid the vagaries of local market, the cash buyers and the yard owners prefer to consume time by notifying the Competent Authority just a few hours before the next available beaching tide to rise.[106] A beaching tide is a contingent event mostly depends on natural phenomena and does not occur every day in every week.[107] These circumstances inevitably place acute time pressure even upon the inspection team of the regulatory agency that eventually leads to a cursory or no inspections being done.[108] There seems to be no mechanism to anatomize the term *'due time'* that appears in 2011 Rule. Eventually the recyclers and the cash buyers remain the key persons to decide when and how much time to offer to the regulatory authorities for ship's inspection or whether to frustrate the process entirely keeping virtually no tangible accountability whatsoever either of the EOL shipowners namely the cash buyers or the ship recyclers.

Subject to the prescribed formalities, the rule has set a strict time frame of only two working days for beaching[109] and breaking permission[110] to be granted. It has also been designed to streamline the boarding process on an expedited basis. These expediting mechanisms although is designed to increase business efficiency[111] of ship recyclers, may adversely affect the quality of screening required by the rule. It is feared that, the breakneck speed in the process of detection without any safeguards addressing the capacity and resources could result in a perfunctory job.

---

[106]Usually, the tidal time scale in Chittagong is every 6 hours. However, the high tide that is suitable for beaching comes in average 3 to 4 times a month. Interview with Captain Anam Chowdhury, Beaching Master and Advisor, Bangladesh Ship Breakers Association (BSBA), Chittagong (Aug. 4, 2016) [hereinafter Captain Anam Interview].
See also Tide-Forecast (2018), "Beaching is the process in which a ship is laid on a tidal mudflat. The vessel is grounded deliberately during high tide popularly called as beaching tide. The ship breaking operations usually take place during low tide when the vessel is not submerged by the sea" (Captain Anam Interview).
www.tide-forecast.com/locations/Chittagong-Bangladesh/tides/latest.
See also www.alangtradeguide.com/TideTable.aspx.

[107]Captain Anam Interview.

[108]Ali Shahin Interview.

[109]*Id.* at Rule 9.7.

[110]*Id.* at Rule 11(viii).

[111]Interview with Md. Mokbul Hossain, Director Department of Environment Chittagong Division, Chittagong (Aug. 4, 2016) [hereinafter Mokbul Hossain Interview].

The Position of New and Existing Ship Under SBRR 2011:

An ocean-going ship built with hazardous substances in its structure poses environmental issues proportionately at the end of its life when they are dismantled. It is therefore also necessary to regulate ship builders and ensure that they avoid using the unnecessary hazardous substances at the stage of construction of ships in a ship building facility. The 2011 rule does not forbid new installation of any hazardous material in the structure of a new ship at any shipbuilding facility in the country or a dry dock while repairing an existing ship at any port facility or offshore terminal irrespective of the flag of the vessel. This omission apparently covers the ships destined for recycling only. New and operating ships, both foreign and local, are excluded from the jurisdiction of SBRR 2011.

The Uncertainty With Downstream Waste Management:

Generation of numerous types of hazardous waste is a natural consequence of ship dismantling in any facility. These downstream toxic substances must be removed timely from the facility and disposed of in an environmentally sound manner through a well-managed downstream waste management system in other words through an authorized Treatment Storage and Disposal Facility (TSDF). The 2011 rule did not include this inseparable downstream waste management work as part of the ship recycling activity.[112] However under the 2011 rule when applying for a ship recycling facility plan (SRFP) every ship recycling facility (SRF) must have an existing membership with a pre-registered treatment, storage, and disposal facility (TSDF) operator.[113] Currently, there is no TSDF facility authorized by the government of Bangladesh,[114] and according to recent SENSREC report more than 150 SRFs have been au-

[112]*Id.* at Rule 2 (x).
[113]*Id.* at Rule 15.1 (b). *Note* that SBSR 2011 is fully enforced since December 2011 and 165 SRF has been authorized by the MoI. However, as of now no TSDF operator has been operating in the country. However, the MoI is undergoing 2nd Phase of SENSREC project that covers TSDF which is now ongoing.
[114]Interview with Mizanur Rahman, National Project Manager, IMO SENSREC Project, Deputy Secretary, MOI, Dhaka, Bangladesh (Aug. 1, 2016).

thorized.[115] It is therefore apparent that the SBRR 2011 has failed to provide an interim measure for the authorization of the SRF pending these essential services are set up by the government.[116]

The EOL Ships: a Hazardous Waste or Hazardous Material?

The rule did not make any sensible distinction between the terms; '*hazardous waste*' and '*hazardous material*' which are completely different objects and governed by different international regimes.[117] A substance attributed as 'hazardous waste', as opposed to 'hazardous material', attracts complex prohibitory jurisdiction of the Basel Convetion.[118] The SBRR 2011 without regard has used these keywords interchangeably.[119] Even the word 'waste' has got different meanings in different jurisdictions, and the international law is still struggling to settle this definitional issue.[120] Apparently, the definition of 'hazardous waste' is far from settled in international law.[121] SBRR 2011 is essentially a transnational regime with significant international impact and the ability to govern the activities of international actors beyond the domestic territory.[122] An inconsistent use of core terminologies may contribute to an irreconcilable transnational jurisprudence on the cross-border movement of goods, waste and hazardous waste alike.

[115]Shahadat Hossain, M. Sharifuzzaman, & SR Chowdhury, *Environmental impact of the ship recycling industry in Bangladesh*, Final Report for Imo Sensrec Project Phase 1 11 (2016), www.imo.org/en/OurWork/Environment/MajorProjects/Pages/Ship-recycling.aspx (hereinafter IMO Environmental Impact Study SENSREC Project).

[116]It therefore seems that all the SRF authorized currently by the Government are operating without fulfilling the prerequisite of the authorization of the SRF under the SBRR 2011.

[117]*Id.* at Rule 2 (xix).

[118]Ishtiaque Ahmed, The Basel Convention on the Control of Transboundary Movements of Hazardous Wastes and Their Disposal: A Legal Misfit in Global Ship Recycling Jurisprudence, 29 Wash. Int'l L.J. 426 (2020).

[119]*Id.* at Rule 2 (xv).

[120]Ahmed, *supra* note 86 at 440-442

[121]*Id.*

[122]Carrie Menkel-Meadow, *Why and How to Study "Transnational" Law*, 1 UC Irvine L. Rev. no. 1 110-111 (2011), www.law.uci.edu/lawreview/Vol1No1Articles/menkelmeadow.pdf.

Ship Recycling Facility Plan (SRFP):

The rule recognizes that the handling of asbestos is a major area of concern.[123] It requires all yard owners to construct ACM (Asbestos Containing Materials) and a negative pressure chamber.[124] However, it's not mandatory for yards having asbestos containment capacity less than 100 metric tons.[125] A scrap ship on average contains 15,000 pounds (approximately seven and one half tons) of asbestos.[126] Depending on size and capacity, each yard dismantles up to three ships on average per year.[127] On the other hand, hazardous waste cannot be stored in a facility more than ninety days after production.[128] In practice, there would hardly be any need for any yard owners to use and maintain negative pressure chambers of 100-ton capacity for asbestos management at the facility, as required by law.[129] It is apparent that a substandard facility with minimal investment in safety may still qualify without violating the standard set by the rule. The rule also did not make any attempt to eliminate or reduce the manual labor that has been supporting the industry in South Asia since the 1980s.

Authorization of Ship Recycling Facility

Before being authorized, a SRF is required to submit an undertaking about its safety, health and environmental management system,[130] its commitment to continuos improvement,[131] identification of rules and responsibilities of the personnel engaged in it,[132] and emergency preparedness,[133] or a system of monitoring the performance by safety offi-

[123]SBRR 2011 Rule 16.1(x).

[124]*Id.* at Rule 18(iii).

[125]*Id.* at Rule 16.1(x).

[126]Syed Tashfin Chowdhury, *Graveyard shift: Dismantling toxic ships in Bangladesh,* Independent (July 26, 2013), www.independent.co.uk/news/world/asia/graveyard-shift-dismantling-toxic-ships-in-bangladesh-8734375.html.
See also ILO (2018), www.ilo.org/safework/info/WCMS_110335/lang--en/index.htm.

[127]Interview with Md Abu Taher, President of Bangladesh Ship Breakers and Recyclers Association (BSBRA), Zhoushan, China (July 25, 2019).

[128]HWR 2011 Rule 20(3).

[129]SBRR 2011 Rules 16.1(x), & 17.19

[130]*Id.* at Rule 15.6.

[131]*Id.* at Rule 15.6 (b).

[132]*Id.* at Rule 15.6 (c). The Rule does not clarify how this cancellation is different than a mere suspension if the authorization can be legally reinstated on addressing the shortcomings.

[133]*Id.* at Rule 15.6 (e).

cers.[134] However, it is not clear, how a violation could legally be assessed, as there has been no attempt to set any specific obligation concerning any of the above activities, including the deadline within which these undertakings are to be in compliance.

The Enforcement Strategy Under SBRR 2011

In any event, the cancellation of the permit is restricted to non-compliance with agreed conditions of authorization by the SRFP.[135] The approval can be legally reinstated by addressing the shortcomings.[136] There is no consequence for any past violations. This flexibility may not contribute in discouraging breach and a scrupulous owner of an SRF may be tempted to wait until the faults are detected by the regulatory agencies. Apparently, there is also no mechanism that guarantees regular inspection of the facility directly on the part of the Competent Authority.

Import of End of Life Ship

An EOL ship often creates a situation of *'fait accomli'*[137] on its arrival.[138] DoE[139] apparently is in a better position to judge environmental issues while issuing the NOC[140] before its imports, but steered clear from such an important process by the 2011 rule. NGOs have adduced much evidence of fraud committed by cash buyers[141] regarding the precleaning of ships prior to sending them to Bangladesh.[142] There has been no attempt to incorporate this expertise in the policy making process by

[134]*Id.* at Rule 15.6 (f).

[135]*Id.* at Rule 15.4.

[136]*Id.*

[137]*'fait accomli'*is a French legal term which means a thing that has already happened or been decided before those affected hear about it, leaving them with no option but to accept it. See www.dictionary.com/browse/fait-accompli

[138]SS Norway.

[139]Department of Environment

[140]No Objection Certificates

[141]Once a vessel reaches the end of its service life, most ship owners sell their vessel to a so-called cash buyer. Cash buyers are companies that specialize in the trade of end-of-life vessels, and most - if not all - sales of end-of-life ships to beaching yards in South Asia

[142]Rizwana Hasan, *Corporate Crime & State Responsibility The Case of Ship Breaking*, UNTNC 15-17 (Oct., 2016), www.ohchr.org/Documents/HRBodies/HRCouncil/WGTransCorp/Session2/PanelIIISubtheme2/RizwanaHassan.pdf.

the government. Filing a dispute in a court regarding the hazardous status of a vessel at the point of entry into the facility, leading to an arrest of a ship, has been an ongoing phenomenon in the current ship recycling market in Bangladesh.[143]

Pre-Cleaning of End of Life Ships

Before exporting an EOL ship, the SBRR 2011 does not require the ship owners to remove additional oil from the bunker tanks that are not essential for ship's last journey to the recycling facility.[144] As such, the rule permits the cleaning process to take place entirely on the beach.[145] Similarly, except tanker, there is no requirement for the issuance of a gas-free certificate for hot work at anchorage.[146] Hence, such certifications and laborious cleaning operations are not effectually prohibited at the inter-tidal part of the beach. The tidal differences in the coastal belt of Chittagong, Bangladesh is one of the highest in the world.[147] When ships are dismantled on the open beach, toxic substances are released from the ship's mass while dismantling operations take place, and are then washed away with semidiurnal waves, inevitably reaching the marine environment.

Ship Recycling Plan

The Ship Recycling Plan (SRP) is a ship-specific document that covers the detailed planning and sequence of the cutting process.[148] This document is prepared by yard owners based on the information on hazardous materials supplied by the Master of the vessel.[149] Its purpose is to ensure, whether a certain facility can safely manage the hazardous wastes to be generated from recycling a certain ship. The SBRR 2011 is not clear at which stage the SRP would be prepared. Given beaching is a non-re-

---

[143]Jago News desk, *HC bans breaking MT Producer ship over radiation fear*, JAGONEWS24.COM (Aug. 29, 2017), www.jagonews24.com/en/national/news/29839.

[144]SBRR 2011 Rules 12, 10.1, 16, 7(a), 19(b), Annexure III.

[145]*Id.* at Rule 10.1.

[146]*Id.* at Rule 9.8, Annexure II.

[147]Press Correspondent, 'Ship breaking: Call for proper waste management', *The Express Tribune*, 18 August 2015, www.tribune.com.pk/story/939892/ship-breaking-call-for-proper-waste-management/ (accessed 10 April 2018)

[148]SBRR 2011 at Rule 16.

[149]*Id.* at Rule 16.1(ii).

versible process,[150] the rule presumes that all authorized SRFs are readily capable of handling all types of ships with any amount of hazardous waste both inbuilt and onboard without reservation. Therefore, if the amount of hazardous wastes is found to be unmanageable in a specific yard due to the lack of its infrastructural capability, this may end up with a catastrophe.

On the other hand, the rule has imposed exorbitant penalty against shipowners or their agents for false declaration of hazardous waste found to be unmanageable for the yard owners after non reversible beaching.[151] But it is unclear how this penalty would be enforced against a foreign ship owner who has concluded a deal of sale and the local agent may not be capable to satisfy such a huge financial penalty in practice.

Safe System of Work

The workplace at the ship recycling yards offers some unique challenges. Unlike ship building, there is no commitment to profit by the skill of naval architects likely to employ scientific methods in ship recycling.[152]The myriad of circumstances in which the workers find themselves while dismantling ships often poses unreasonable risk-taking. Moreover, the rule requires cranes to be tested on regular intervals and constant supervision is required while heavy loads are lifted by cranes.[153] Unfortunately, the rule does not explain how to use cranes alongside the ship on the soft, moving, muddy beach where they are actually needed. The rule did not clarify the specific use of the crane at beaching facilities.[154]

In SBRR 2011, there is no requirement to set up any permanent fire-fighting infrastructure and the rule has put substantial reliance on portable fire extinguishers.[155] The Rule relies heavily on the informal neighborhood assistance.[156]An emergency response system relying on unorga-

[150]SBRR 2011 Rule 6.
[151]*Id.* at Rule 46.12. The penalty is one crore (Equivalent to USD 125,000).
[152]K. S. Iqbal et al., *An Approach to Safer Ship Breaking: The Role of Naval Architects,* Department of Naval Architecture and Marine Engineering Bangladesh Univ. Of Engineering and Technology (Jan. 17, 2012), www.name.buet.ac.bd/ShipBreakingandRecyclingSeminar17012012.pdf (Seminar on Ship Breaking and Ship Recycling in Bangladesh and Compliance with International Regulations).
[153]SBRR 2011 Rule 17.19(f).
[154]Only used at the yard gate for loading of processed scrapped metal over the truck.
[155]SBRR 2011 Rule 17.20.
[156]SBRR 2011 Rule 30.3 (b).

nized, untrained voluntary workers from the neighboring populace may be inadequate when needed.

It is apparent that the SBRR 2011 was adopted in the face of mounting criticism against lawlessness in the governance of this pollution-heavy industry in Bangladesh. This was followed by the order of the High Court Division of the Supreme Court of Bangladesh in a Writ Petition that compelled the government to adopt the rule hastily within a specified timeframe.[157] Evidently, in absence of a settled independent regulatory agency, there was a severe lack of effective competition within this industry in Bangladesh and the potential for the undue exercise of market power was considerable.[158] NGOs have reported that in any stage of the law making process in both the SBRR 2011 and the SRA 2018, little or no substantive consultations took place with relevant stake holders such as environmental or labour activists.[159] In their adoption processes and in the legislative texts, no reflection of any of the long standing and established general principles of environmental laws such as polluter pay principle, proximity principle, precautionary principle or common and differentiated responsibility have been noticeable.

Furthermore, under the international law on ship recycling, namely the HKC, the Competent Authority is a governmental regulatory agency.[160] A regulatory agency is a public body responsible for exercising autonomous power over some areas of human activity in a supervisory role. Regulatory agencies or authorities are commonly established to enforce standard of safety and to protect the consumers in a market with lack of fair competition or the potential for the excessive or undue use of market power. Regulatory agencies are therefore typically part of the executive branch of the government and have received their power from the legislative branch. Their actions are generally open to scrutiny by way of judicial review. Under the BSRA 2018, the governing bodies of the Competent Authority for the ship recycling in Bangladesh namely the BSRB is formed by 13 members of the board where at least three members are appointed by the government who represents ship recycling industry[161] who are the subject of governance by the BSRB. Given only one third board members are required to form the quorum as per the BSRA 2018 for a meeting to be valid in the board level and no quorum is

[157]Ishtiaque Ahmed, Unravelling Socio-Economic and Ecological Distribution Conflicts in Ship-breaking in Bangladesh for Addressing Negative Externalities in Law and Policy Making, 29 Minn. J. Int'l L. 206 (2020).

[158]Id at 194

[159]Id at 207

[160]HKC Art 2.3

[161]Bangladesh Ship Recycling Act 2018, Sec 10

required in the adjourned meetings[162] there is a significant cause for concern about the optimum functioning of this regulatory agency. Attaining sustainability in this industry in Bangladesh using these questionable legal provisions may prove to be a difficult exercise.

Vii. Worker's Rights in Ship Breaking Industry in Bangladesh

The supreme law that governs the right of workers against their employers in Bangladesh is the Labour Act 2006 (LA 2006). Under this law, a shipbreaking yard is an industrial establishment[163] as well as a factory where production process is carried on.[164] This Act applies to the ship breaking workers.

Conditions of Employment

The 2011 rule imposes considerable penalty upon the yard owners for engaging uncertified workers[165], women workers,[166] and underaged workers.[167] The same rule applies to the workers supplied by contractors.[168] However, as far as the employment rights of the workers, provided by contractors, are concerned, the SBRR 2011 is silent, and Labour Act 2006 (LA 2006) imposes this obligation upon the current employers,[169]which in the ship breaking sector is mostly the contractors.[170] Under the recent amendment of the Labour Act 2006, establishment of any contractor and subcontractor engaged in shipbreaking

[162]Bangladesh Ship Recycling Act 2018, Sec 12(6)
[163]Bangladesh Labor Act 2006 [hereinafter LA 2006] § 2(61)(i), www.bdlaws.minlaw.gov.bd/bangla_sections_detail.php?id=952&sections_id=29070.
[164]The requirement is satisfied if the facility uses at least five workers on any day of the year.
[165]SBRR 2011 Rule 46.
[166]*Id.* at Rule 45.5.
[167]*Id.* at Rule 46.4.
[168]*Id.* at Rule 17.1.
[169]LA 2006 § 161, www.bdlaws.minlaw.gov.bd/bangla_sections_detail.php?id=952&sections_id=29400.
[170]Almost all workers are recruited by the contractors on day basis. *See* Ship Breaking Bangladesh (2012), www.shipbreakingbd.info/overview.html.

is also a separate and independent industrial organization[171] and is accountable for all its actions as an employer. The Labour Rule 2015 (LR 2015) enacted under the power granted in LA 2006 confirms that a contractor's establishment is a separate and independent organization.[172] However, the temporary employment practice makes it easy for the yard owners to shift many substantive obligations to the workers upon the contractors and the subcontractors. As per the LA 2006, the yard owners do not have to take the financial liability to compensate workers if a casualty is resulted from a breach of contract or the negligence of the contractor.[173] The remedy of workers for compensation on death and injury may practically lie in most cases to the contractors only.[174] This is a significant possibility as contractors are the principal supervising authorities for the workers who owe primary duties to supply PPE and training for their workers under the latest amendment of LA 2006.[175]

To obtain a registration, a contractor is required to be solvent and requires executing a bond or surety.[176] The security deposit for a contractor's establishment able to supply workers up to hundred is only BDT 200,000 (USD 2,500 approximately).[177]Although license fees are charged as per the nature of establishment such as a shop, restaurant, factory, bank or an insurance company but there is no such distinction is made between a hazardous industry like ship breaking and others.[178] A ship breaking yard has therefore been considered in equal term with non-hazardous industry like bank, restaurant, food court, hair salon or a departmental store where the question of compensation for loss of life or limb is hardly relevant. The question of financial liability arising out of coastal pollution in beach breaking is crucial but how such miniature establishments would bear all such great liabilities pose many impenetrable questions.

---

[171]LA 2006 § 2(61) Labor Act (Amendment) (2013), www.bdlaws.minlaw.gov.bd/bangla_sections_detail.php?id=952&sections_id=29070.

[172]Bangladesh Labour Rules 2015 [hereinafter BLR 2015] Rule 10.4.

[173]*Id.*

[174]According to the current report, ongoing wages of the workers are not an issue, but the works and their family members face a severe struggle in recovering the concession on death or permanent injuries.

[175]Under the LA 2006, except compensation for death and injury and the issue of training the employers do not appear to hold any responsibility for the workers supplied by the contractors.

[176]BLR 2015 Rule 11

[177]BLR 2015 Schedule 7. In a ship breaking field, each contractor supplies 50 to 100 workers, and there may remain several contractors engaged at a time (Interview).

[178]*Id.* Schedule.

To confer same right as a regular worker, the term 'temporary workers' has recently been included in the definition of "worker" under the latest amendment of LA 2006.[179] A wide range of rights, widely claimed by the industry, are now readily available to the workers of the ship breaking industries who mostly are temporary workers.[180] These include right to have a service book,[181] an appointment letter, ID card with photos,[182] overtime payment,[183] casual leave, medical leave, sick leave, yearly holiday with wages, festival holidays, ad-hoc or unpaid wages and many more. There are also special provisions for welfare, dispute resolution, right to form a trade union, restrictions on recruitment of children and adolescent labors, etc.

Apparently, the ship breaking workers are now favored with many substantive rights, but most of such rights are tied to the status of permanent employment. The benefits are measured according to the duration of service within a closed loop of a year or one-half year of continuous service. The SBRR 2011 does not mandate employing permanent workers irrespective of the financial ability of the yard owners. As noted earlier, over 70% are migrant workers who mostly arrive from the northern and impoverished part of the country.[184]

A worker may not also be able to work with the same contractor every day.[185] The service book that contains essential rights such as the service

---

179LA 2006 § 4(1), 4(4), 4(5), www.bdlaws.minlaw.gov.bd/bangla_sections_detail.php?id=952&sections_id=29072.
LA 2006 § 2(65), www.bdlaws.minlaw.gov.bd/bangla_sections_detail.php?id=952&sections_id=29070.

180*Id.*

181*Id.* at § 5, www.bdlaws.minlaw.gov.bd/bangla_sections_detail.php?id=952&sections_id=29074.

182*Id.*

183*Id.* at § 108, www.bdlaws.minlaw.gov.bd/bangla_sections_detail.php?id=952&sections_id=29435.

184Midori N. Courtice et al., *Asbestos-Related Disease in Bangladeshi Ship Breakers: A Pilot Study*, Int'l J. Occupational & Environmental Health 144, www.researchgate.net/publication/307748389_Asbestos-Related_Disease_in_Banlgadeshi_Ship_Breakers_A_Pilot_Study.

185Interview with Mohammad Nazim Uddin, Joint Convener, Ship Breaking Trade Union Forum, Chittagong (Aug. 10, 2016) [hereinafter Nazim, Uddin Interview] *also* Shahin Interview, *supra* note 7. *Also* E-mail from Nicola Mulinaris, Communication and Policy Officer, NGO Shipbreaking Platform, Brussels, Belgium (Mar. 21, 2016).

record, performance and experience[186] is reserved for the permanent workers and not available for the temporary workers under the LA 2006.[187] Under Sec.100 of the LA 2006, the regular working hours are forty-eight per week.[188] If any worker works more than forty-eight hours in each week, he is entitled to receive overtime benefit which is almost twice than his regular pay rate.[189] The maximum permitted hours are eight hours in a day with two hours overtime permitted subject to section 108 of the LA 2006.[190] Hence, if a worker can work for four days with ten hours in each day of a given week,[191] it would remain up to the discretion of contractors whether to pay him overtime wage or not. This is unlikely, as calculating a six-day slot of the week, a worker may not fulfill the forty-eight hours threshold in each week. Similarly, the provisions on weekly holiday do not assist temporary workers as they may be operated under different contractors on different days of the week.

Few substantive benefits become due when a worker completes six months continuous service, and other requires one year under a single employer in a given calendar year.[192] For example to get compensation as a leased worker,[193] to earn ten days casual leave annually with pay,[194] to receive fourteen days sick leave in a year[195] and leave with pay

---

[186]LA 2006 § 7, www.bdlaws.minlaw.gov.bd/bangla_sections_detail.php?id=952&sections_id=29075.

[187]*Id.* at § 6, www.bdlaws.minlaw.gov.bd/bangla_sections_detail.php?id=952&sections_id=29074.

[188]*Id.* at § 102(1), www.bdlaws.minlaw.gov.bd/bangla_sections_detail.php?id=952&sections_id=29429.

[189]*Id.* at § 108(1), www.bdlaws.minlaw.gov.bd/bangla_sections_detail.php?id=952&sections_id=29435.

[190]*Id.* at § 100, www.bdlaws.minlaw.gov.bd/bangla_sections_detail.php?id=952&sections_id=29427.

[191]Many workers in ship breaking field work in average 10 hours a day under the contractors. *See* Where do the "floating dustbins" end up? FIDH, p20 and p38 www.fidh.org/IMG/pdf/bd1112a.pdf

[192]LA 2006 § 14, www.bdlaws.minlaw.gov.bd/bangla_sections_detail.php?id=952&sections_id=29082.

[193]*Id.* at § 16(1), www.bdlaws.minlaw.gov.bd/bangla_sections_detail.php?id=952&sections_id=29158.

[194]Id. at § 117 (1), www.bdlaws.minlaw.gov.bd/bangla_sections_detail.php?id=952&sections_id=29444.

[195]*Id.* at § 115, www.bdlaws.minlaw.gov.bd/bangla_sections_detail.php?id=952&sections_id=29443.

benefit,[196] a worker must complete one-year continuous service under a same employer.[197] These benefits are also tied to a given calendar year and expressly made non-cumulative i.e. nontransferable to the following year.[198]

Again to be entitled to compensation for death while in service, the worker must be in continuous service for two years preceding to his death as a permanent worker.[199] To be compensated for an occupational decease suffered in the facility, the worker must serve for that establishment for at least six months consecutively.[200] In a ship-breaking facility at least twelve percent of workers suffer from asbestos-related disease.[201]Very few of the workers would pass this consecutive day of service requirement. Moreover, there is a long latency period and most of the occupational diseases that are common in these toxic industries may develop after long time of exposure to toxic conditions.[202] There would also be no scope for joint liability between the employers even if the disease had developed over years of working in two or more facilities if the duration of service with each employer is less than six months which happens most frequently. Hence in the absence of any requirement to recruit permanent workers, there is every incentive to hire temporary workers as they hardly have anything to claim other than their daily wages. Under the LA 2006, if the number of permanent workers exceeds one hundred, the employer is bound to purchase group insurance policy for the workers.[203] Moreover, there is no hard and fast rule to dismiss temporary workers by the employers who as per the law can be hired and

---

[196]*Id.* at § 118(1), www.bdlaws.minlaw.gov.bd/bangla_sections_detail.php?id=952&sections_id=29445.

[197]*Id.* at § 115, www.bdlaws.minlaw.gov.bd/bangla_sections_detail.php?id=952&sections_id=29435.

[198]*Id.*

[199]*Id.* at § 19, www.bdlaws.minlaw.gov.bd/bangla_sections_detail.php?id=952&sections_id=30089.

[200]*Id.* at § 150(3)(b).

[201]Tarek Mahmud, *Asbestos: The slow poison killing ship-breaking workers*, Dhaka Tribune (Feb. 3, 2017), www.dhakatribune.com/bangladesh/environment/2017/02/02/asbestos-slow-poison-killing-ship-breaking-workers/.

[202]Mesotheleoma (2018), www.mesotheliomaguide.com/mesothelioma/symptoms/latency-period/.

[203]*Id.* at § 99 (1), www.bdlaws.minlaw.gov.bd/bangla_sections_detail.php?id=952&sections_id=29981.

fired at will without any compensation or notice whatsoever which does not apply to the permanent workers under the LA 2006.[204]

Child and Adoslescent Work

Under the LA 2006, there is a complete prohibition of child labor in any industry in Bangladesh.[205] However adolescents can be recruited if a medical certificate or birth certificate is kept in the custody of the employer,[206] and the adolescent must be supervised by an adult competent person at work.[207] Hazardous activities in Bangladesh are listed by the government time to time by gazette notifications.[208] Ship-breaking has been classified as one of the most hazardous activities vide Sec 68 of the Labor Rule 2015.[209] Under the SBRR 2011, the recruitment of both child and adolescent has been completely prohibited [210]also included are women workers.[211] Under the SBRR 2011 the financial penalty against yard owners for appointing a worker below eighteen is BDT 75,000 (Equivalent to USD 950) per worker.[212] This is a considerable amount in the economic market of Bangladesh given child labor and adolescent works are ubiquitous in Bangladesh with no practical barrier in the field.[213] The extreme poverty connected to family backgrounds having no social security from the government prevents these laws from being enforced strictly. There is in fact no shortage of avenues to hide away even if caught red-handed. Corruption is widely prevalent across the coun-

[204]Under the LA 2006 Sec 20, the employment contract between a temporary worker with his employer is a 'contract at will.' Therefore, the remaining provisions even have no bearing on the length of service are also quite vulnerable to them.

[205]LA 2006 § 34 (1), www.bdlaws.minlaw.gov.bd/bangla_sections_detail.php?id=952&sections_id=26435.

[206]*Id.*

[207]*Id.* at § 40.1, www.bdlaws.minlaw.gov.bd/bangla_sections_detail.php?id=952&sections_id=26441.

[208]*Id.* at § 39 (1), 39 (2), www.bdlaws.minlaw.gov.bd/bangla_sections_detail.php?id=952&sections_id=26440.

[209]BLR 2015 § 68.

[210]SBRR 2011 Rule 46.4. The Majority Act of 1875 Bangladesh describes a person to be a child below 18 years.

[211]*Id.* at Rule 46.5.

[212]*Id.* at Rule 46.4.

[213]UNICEF, *Child Labor in Bangladesh*, 2 at 2, www.clu-mole.gov.bd/img/pdf_file/dfb80c434ccef8400e70c78f85c6e5a2.pdf (last visited Apr. 18, 2020).

try[214] and ship-breaking industry is not an exception. Many children or adolescents are raised by single parents or have lost their father; the only source of income. Understandably, all these incidents are coined by poverty and hunger, not by any gain or profit. Interestingly under the LA 2006, the parents of the child workers may also be penalized.[215] Contrary to the LA 2006, the SBRR 2011 has been quite loud on the issue of child and adolescent labor but remains mum in addressing the real problem on the ground; submission of a fake certificate as a proof of age by the employers. It appears that the regulatory authorities in Bangladesh hardly control the influx of children at ship breaking yards and there is every chance to employ adolescent workers in a ship-breaking yard by disguising the age without any practical consequence against the yard owners.[216] The report of NGO reveals that up to twenty five percent workers are adolescent across the shipbreaking industry currently in Bangladesh.[217]

Workers Union

Traditionally, the politicians in Bangladesh have used the trade union as one of the ways and means to achieve their political dreams.[218] The Fair Labor Association reports that, in 2002, in Bangladesh only three percent of workers were affiliated with trade union and among them the majority

[214]*Corruption Perception Index 2019,* Transparency International, www.transparency.org/cpi2019 (last visited Mar. 3, 2018).

[215]LA 2006 § 285, www.bdlaws.minlaw.gov.bd/bangla_sections_detail.php?id=952&sections_id=26339.

[216]Wendy Laursen, *Is There Child Labour in Shipbreaking Yards?*, The Maritime Executive (Sept. 4, 2015), www.maritime-executive.com/features/Is-There-Child-Labor-in-Shipbreaking-Yards-2014-08-05 (last visited Apr. 18, 2020).

[217]NGO Shipbreaking Platform, *Substandard shipbreaking: a global challenge*, Brussels 5 (Feb. 2017), www.shipbreakingplatform.org/shipbrea_wp2011/wp-content/uploads/2017/01/Worldwide-overview_FINAL_2017.pdf.

[218]Subramaniyam Arumugam, Nimalathasan Balasundaram, *Industrial Relation System: Lessons for Bangladesh and Sri Lanka from Japanese Perspective*, LXII Petroleum-Gas University Of Ploiesti Bulletin, Economic Sciences Series no. 1 54-55 (2010), www.researchgate.net/publication/200717466_Industrial_Relation_System_Lessons_for_Bangladesh_and_Sri_Lanka_from_Japanese_Perspectives.

were closely affiliated with national politics,[219] having less involvement with economically active population at work. Almost 75 to 80 percent of those workers belong to the informal sector in Bangladesh.[220] The majority of these low profile, financially active people lack formal education,[221] and are often dominated by the politicians in the country[222] on whose clemency their leaders depend for personal gain with no practical benefit to these ordinary workers. On the other hand, it has been revealed that 90% of the established employers belong to the owner's association,[223] unfettered from national politics. The businesspersons, instead, dominate the politics as most of the members of Parliament in Bangladesh traditionally are high profile business icons.[224] LA 2006 is infiltrated with severe flaws identified by the ILO which has recommended immediate reform in the collective bargaining process.[225] However, all these fell on deaf ears as the government has traditionally played a double role. The government says workers are free to join trade unions as per their choice, but maneuvered the law in such a way that implementing collective bargaining in the real sense has remained infructuous.[226]

LA 2006 has conferred equal rights to both employers and employees to form and join unions and elect their representatives in full freedom to pursue their common goals.[227] To enjoy such rights, an employer is no different than an employee. Traditionally, however a broken chain of command exists between workers and their unions mostly because of some complicated socio, economic, and cultural equations and political belief that isolate them more swiftly. Under the LA 2006, there is no

---

[219]*Annual Public Report Part 4 of 4,* Fair Labor Organization 247 (Aug. 18, 2004),
www.fairlabor.org/sites/default/files/documents/reports/2004_annual_public_report_part4.pdf.

[220]*Id.* at 248. Cited in *ICFTU Bangladesh: Annual Survey of Violations of Trade Union Rights 2003,*
www.icftu.org/displaydocument.asp?Index=991217710&Language=EN.

[221]A. Ghose, N. Majid, C. Ernst, *The Global Employment Challenge,* International labour Office, Geneva, Academic Foundation, 2008, p.21

[222]Andrew Brown, Jane Hutchison (ed.), Organizing *Labour in Globalizing Asia,* Routledge, 2003, 34

[223]Bangladesh Employer's Federation, [website], 2020, www.bef.org.bd/about-us-2/

[224]Nizam Ahmed, *Jatiya Sangsad: The Parliament of Bangladesh,*
www.psa.ac.uk/sites/default/files/Parliament%20of%20Bangladesh.pdf. Also see www.thedailystar.net/bangladesh-national-election-2018/news/its-businessmens-parliament-again-1672930

[225]Annual Public Report, *supra* note 191, at 247-248.

[226]*Id.*

[227]LA 2006 § 176.

threshold in the number of labor unions that can be formed in an organization. On the other hand, the law requires at least 30% of worker participation in the registration of a trade union.[228] Observance of this broken culture followed by ill-disposed legal provisions makes it difficult in practice to unite them and fulfill the minimum quantitative requirement for registration. Moreover, until the registration is complete, any function of union is prohibited by law[229] and the code is silent about the preparatory activities directed to form a new union. This gap in law has traditionally been abused by the employers in many industries in Bangladesh including the ship-breaking, extensively to dismiss a worker attempting to begin talking about a labor union with other co-workers within a business establishment.[230] ILO committee of expert considers the issue as a severe restriction of the worker's ability of collective bargaining and to form a union as per their choice which needs immediate reform.[231] It has oftentimes been reported that employees have been persecuted personally by deploying police to their residence.[232]

In fact, the contracts of the contractors with the yard owners often do not last long and mostly ship specific.[233]A meaningful trade union in such a bizarre circumstance is virtually unimaginable. It appears that government has traditionally attempted to use the power of lawmaking and the instrument of law to maintain a status quo thereby legalizing the vulnerable position of the workers in general.

Worker's Right To Strike

Employees have the right to protect their economic interest through strike. Industrial Relations Ordinance 1969 (Ordinance no XXIII of 1969) recognizes such right.[234] However, the condition of freedom of

---

[228]*Id.* at § 179(2).
[229]*Id.* at § 192, 233.
[230]Interview with Rizwanur Rahman Khan, Joint Secretary General, Bangladesh Free Trade Union Congress, Chittagong, Bangladesh (Aug. 5, 2016) [hereinafter Rizwanur Rahman Interview].
[231]ILO (2018), www.ilo.org/global/about-the-ilo/newsroom/statements-and-speeches/WCMS_218067/lang--en/index.htm. *See also* UN Agency news, *Revised Bangladesh labour law 'falls short' of international standards*, UN News (July 22, 2013), https://news.un.org/en/story/2013/07/445222-revised-bangladesh-labour-law-falls-short-international-standards-un-agency.
[232]Annual Public Report *supra* note 191.
[233]Interview with AM Nazim Uddin, Joint Convener, Bangladesh Institute of Labour Studies Chittagong, Chittagong, Bangladesh (Aug. 5, 2016).
[234]Industrial Relations Ordinance 1969 § 28.

association looks vulnerable under this law where there is a penalty including imprisonment for instigating illegal strike or lock-out or taking part in or instigating a 'go-slow'. The go-slow has been defined under the ordinance as organized, deliberate and purposeful slowing down of standard output of work by a body of workers.[235] The law has defined illegal lockout and strike but not illegal go-slow. Go-slow technique is used to persuade an employer to agree to higher pay or better working conditionsusually is a mild version of a strike, it may also be said. So, according to the definition, any attempt to get the employer to agree to higher pay, better working condition, could be interpreted as a go-slow action. These provisions are not difficult to explain in favor of the employers where, irrespective of the justifiability of go-sow, a company can initiate action under the Section 53 of the IRO 1969 (Industrial Relations Ordnance 1969). In a condition of pauperism, mere filing criminal cases irrespective of their merit against workers living hand to mouth is good enough to despoil his entire wherewithal of life with no compensation whatsoever regardless of the outcome of the cases. Also, the words, 'organized', 'deliberate', and 'purposeful' used in IRO 1969 deserve further clarifications to avoid any misuse of power enjoyed by the employers.

Ship recycling is a highly labor-intensive industry with significant rate of casualty record consistently being apparent since 1980s when the industry migrated to the South Asian region.[236] Due to this high risk factor, this industry has attracted some of the most vulnerable classes of people from the most destitute parts of some developing counties of South Asia where the industry has flourished. In both Bangladesh, India and Pakistan there has been a common hallmark of this industry where migrant people from the poorest parts of the country have constituted the main body of the ship recycling workers pool.[237] Almost 98% of the workers of this industry is temporary[238] and this position is unlikely to change soon as most ship breaking facilities by virtue of the very nature of the industry are not engaged in breaking of ships all over the year and the ship-breaking task therefore can be said as intermittent in nature. The part time nature of ship breaking works creates a significant hurdle to create a skilled worker's pool in the industry which undoubtedly forms an essential part of the equation of sustainability of this industry. Due to these special characteristics prevailing in the ship-breaking industry, the

[235]*Id.*at § 59.

[236]MD. Saiful Karim, Shipbreaking in Developing Country, A Requiem for Environmental Justice From The Perspective of Bangladesh 6 (2018).

[237]Ishtiaque Ahmed, *Ungovernable Ships at the End of their Lives and the Response of the Hong Kong Convention: A Critical Appraisal of the Treaty on Shipbreaking from the Perspective of South Asian Ship-breaking Nations*, 18 Santa Clara J. Int'l L. 167 (2020)

[238]Id at 166

mainstream labor law, applicable to all other types of industries in the country, does not go along easily with this most dangerous and labor-intensive industry in the world. As a truly global industry, it would hardly be possible to solve this problem unitarily from a state level. To circumvent this problem the ship-breaking labor regulations should be harmonized among ship recycling states, taking note of the special character and risks involved in ship-breaking works. A separate international regime like the Maritime Labor Convention (MLC) incorporating the special rights of ship-breaking labours may be considered. This may incorporate provisions for the standardization of worker's training and creation of a pool of minimum number of regular workers.

Viii. Environmental Compliance and Monitoring

The Department of Environment is entrusted to issue a yard specific clearance; however, the 2011 rule did not make clear if it is compulsory to release a ship specific clearance before the beaching permission is granted.[239]This silence in law has provided the recyclers of ships opportunities to argue that under the current state of law no environmental clearance is necessary before beaching and recycling of ships.[240]As a result, in a very few cases, the ship specific NOC is applied for by the yard owners.[241]In some areas, overlapping of responsibility between two departments of the government has been apparent. For example, both the DoE and the SRB oftentimes have been entrusted with identical responsibility but with separate accountability to their respective departments. The responsibilities include regular monitoring of air quality, water and soil quality using sample from the site.[242] In those circumstances, which department is primarily accountable to address those issues, has been a debatable issue. As an orange (B) category industry[243] DoE applies the same criteria over the ship breaking industry as applied to all other land-

---

[239]SBRR 2011 Rule 3.3.

[240]Mintu Chowdhury, *Bangladesh shipbreakers contend no need for environmental clearance*, BDNEWS24.COM (Nov. 7, 2016), www.bdnews24.com/bangladesh/2016/11/07/no-need-to-environmental-clearance-say-ship-breakers-in-bangladesh.

[241]*Id.*

[242]SBRR 2011 Rule 18(viii).

[243]MD. Saiful Karim, Shipbreaking in Developing Country A Requiem For Environmental Justice from The Perspective Of Bangladesh 101 (Routledge, London and New York, 2017).

based hazardous industries to collect the sample of water, air, soil, etc.[244] The same method of testing water and soil sediments does not appear to be suitable in the coast based industry, working within semidiurnal mode of tidal water that changes direction in every six hours. The deposits in the intertidal zone of the sea hardly settle down and wash away directly into the ocean body continuously. On the other hand, the SRB is required to carry out the same task of environmental monitoring independently through an industrial & scientific research lab.[245] Interestingly the SBRR 2011 has imposed upon the Competent Authority a hard-hitting duty to evolve the beaching method into a complete pollution free venture with zero tolerance by ongoing environmental monitoring practice followed by scientific data analysis.[246] The rule also has imposed a duty upon the yard owners to support the DoE in their endeavor to the environmental monitoring by supplying adequate logistics, workforce, testing equipment's, vessels, etc.[247] It is noteworthy that an obligation attached with scientific impossibility is unlikely to be enforced in the court of law. Moreover, a regulatory duty that relies solely on the technical and logistical support of the regulatees may also potentially be unsuccessful due to the presence of conflicting interests.

The HWR 2011 implements the Basel Convention in Bangladesh[248] however, unlike the Basel Convention, it applies to the entities dealing with the hazardous waste and hazardous materials alike.[249] These two terms have been interchangeably used with same meaning to impose liability upon the operators of both hazardous waste and hazardous materials in the country.[250] There is no difference made in the content of the

[244]Mokbul Hossain Interview. Noting that shipbreaking despite poses significant threat to the Marine environment, Govt. still has placed the ship breaking into an orange category instead of the red category. For red listed industry according to Bangladesh Environment Conversation Rule 1997, a heightened measure of environmental clearance is required whereas lesser stringer measure is applicable to the orange category industries. In 2009, the Government assured the Supreme Court that it has taken step to upgrade the ship breaking from the Orange B to red category WP 7260 of 2008. *See* BELA v. Government of Bangladesh, Bangladesh Supreme Court Writ Petition (Civil) No. 7260, 4 (2008), www.bdpil.org/assets/uploads/pdf/c86f3-judgement-ship-breaking-7260-of-2008.pdf.

[245]SBRR 2011 Rule 18(viii).

[246]*Id.*

[247]*Id.* at Rule 18(vii).

[248]HWR 2011 Rule 17.

[249]*Id.* at Rules 2(28), 2(30).

[250]*Id.* at Rule 5.

definition.[251] Under the rule, the importer of the hazardous waste or material needs to ensure that actual product corresponds with the description in the document.[252]Any consignment or lot of hazardous material or hazardous waste is illegal unless permitted by the appropriate state authority of Bangladesh or if permission has been obtained by fraud or deception.[253] In violation of this provision, the importer is primarily responsible for taking the consignment of hazardous waste back to the exporter at his own cost within 30 days of arrival at the anchorage.[254] If due to any inevitable reason the shipment is not possible to return, the importer will remain responsible for bearing the total cost of destruction of such waste or materials in Bangladesh.[255] Basel Convention, on the other hand, makes such transaction a criminal offense.[256] The Conference of the Parties (COP) of the Basel Convention has declared the EOL ship as a hazardous waste in its integral form,[257] but the provision of the illegal shipment under Sec 18 of the HWR 2011 does not appear to apply to EOL ships. It is noted that the rule has used the words consignment or lot. Logically it applies to any lot or consignment which can be carried as cargo by a carrier. Hence, it appears that the rule applies to only hazardous wastes or materials when carried as cargo, not the carrier itself when it is the subject matter of import. On the other hand, the procedure to import an EOL ship is mentioned separately under section 19 of the same rule. This makes it more arguable that section 18 does not apply to EOL ships. Section 17 of the HWR 2011 confirms that Basel Convention shall be applied to all import and export of hazardous waste and materials, but the rule is silent if an EOL ship in its intact condition is a hazardous waste and its import for scrapping can itself be considered as a lot or consignment of hazardous waste.

Unlike the Basel Convention, no state to state communication is required in Bangladesh to import any hazardous waste or goods. Seemingly, there is a massive inconsistency in the domestic waste law with the Basel Convention. It can therefore conveniently be argued that the HWR

---

[251]The HWR 2011 has referred the ECA 1995 for definition of the hazardous material but the definition under mimic the definition given of the hazardous waste under Rule 2(30) of the HWR 2011.

[252]HWR 2011 Rule 5(a).

[253]*Id.* at Rule 18(1)(a).

[254]*Id.* at Rule 18 (2).

[255]*Id.* at Rule 18(3).

[256]Basel Convention art. 4.3.

[257]U.N. Environmental Programme, Report on the Conference of the Parties to the Basel Convention on the Control of Transboundary Movement of Hazardous Wastes and Their Disposal, VII/26, U.N. Doc. UNEP/CHW.7/33 (Jan. 25, 2005) (deciding that an EOL ship may become waste as defined in art. 2 of the Basel Convention and simultaneously, it may be defined as a ship under other international rules)., at 419.

2011 applies to the hazardous waste when imported as cargo only and it does not appear to affect an EOL ships with hazardous waste in its embedded structure. None the less, if the convention were strictly followed, it would have been illegal to import EOL ships for recycling in Bangladesh without prior informed consent directly from the state authority of Bangladesh. The rule appears to have made a distinction in case of EOL ships but does not make it clear as to how an EOL ship is different than other hazardous wastes under the Basel Convention. This stand is also inconsistent to the Supreme Court judgment in WP 7602 of 2008, although the court in its later judgment has diluted the rigor of its earlier version and waived the strict requirements of the Basel Convention for EOL ships without acknowledging the matter. Eventually, both the Supreme Court judgment and the HWR 2011 expressly declare that, Basel Convention applies to all hazardous waste including the EOL ships, but their factual position is sharply contradictory to the fundamental provisions of the Basel Convention of which Bangladesh is a state party since 1992.

Ix. Sanction for Violations

Punishment for the violation has been established in ship breaking industry in two different laws; The SBRR 2011 and the BSR Act 2018 (Bangladesh Ship Recycling Act 2018). Unless death or injury by negligence occurs, it seems there is no liability for violating any provision of SBRR 2011. However, the Bangladesh Ship Recycling Board (BSRB) might ask for rectification without any sanction for past wrongful action.[258] In contravention to any provision of the SBRR 2011, the standard sanction remains the suspension of yard activities.[259] There is no penalty for spillage of oil, sludge, hazardous waste to the environment unless the workers are supplied with proper equipment at the time of handling.[260] For many types of violations, the suspension and rectification methods do not sit properly with ultimate objective of the law. For example, if any worker is made to work at a height in a single instance without a safety belt and the job is already performed without any incident of casually, it would still be a definite violation but it is pointless to keep the operation of the SRF suspended until such fault is rectified. Few other penal provisions require fines to be paid to the government treasury

[258]SBRR 2011 Rule 46.7.
[259]*Id.* at Rule 17(14) (iii).
[260]*Id.* at Rule 46.9.

for violations such as using uncertified workers, [261]women,[262] and workers below eighteen,[263] allowing the workers to work at a height after the sunset[264] and false declaration made by the shipowners about hazardous waste that subsequently found unmanageable.[265] It is interesting to note that an action can only be taken against a ship recycler for loss of life and permanent injury of workers and also subject to proving negligence.[266] There is no concept of strict liability or gross negligence or corporate manslaughter known in SBRR 2011. More interestingly an injury below than permanent disability is not actionable per se in 2011 Rule.

Bangladesh Ship Recycling Act 2018 (BSR Act 2018) also has incorporated penal provisions for certain activities carried out without permission from the appropriate authorities of the government[267] including fake document submission in any application process.[268] Apparently, all these punishments are restricted to mere financial penalties that do not seem to be proportional to the offenses and quite insufficient to discourage violations as required by the HKC.[269] For example under SRA 2018 , the maximum financial penalty for offences including non-reversible beaching without obtaining appropriate permission from the BSRB varies from BDT 10 lacs to 30 lacs which are equivalent to USD 12,000 and USD 35,000 respectively per violation.[270] Given the profit margin from recycling of an EOL ship is pretty high[271] , there is no compulsory and fixed penalty of imprisonment available in law against illegal beaching as well as ships beached illegally are not confiscated by the government, the threshold of penalty seems much inferior to the profit obtained generally from such violations. It therefore appears that gaps in the penal provision in the 2018 Act also would unlikely discourage any possible violations.

Because of such inherent loopholes in the domestic framework regulations pertaining to shipbreaking, imbalance of market powers, reluctance of the shipyard owners in following adequate safety standards, inadequate arrangements for training of workers , lack of awareness of safety

[261]*Id*. at Rule 46.3.
[262]*Id*. at Rule 46.5.
[263]*Id*. at Rule 46.4.
[264]*Id*. at Rule 46.10.
[265]*Id*. at Rule 46.12.
[266]*Id*. at Rule 45.3.
[267]SRA 2015 § 21.1(a).
[268]*Id*. at § 21.1(b).
[269]HKC art. 10.3.
[270]§ 26, and § 27 of SRA 2018
[271]Average profit from a Panamax oil tanker with 80,000 DWT is approx. $920,000 see www.marinelink.com/news/economics-scrapping414382

within the ship breaking workers themselves have failed to prevent the gradual rise of workers casualty in ship-breaking sites.[272]

Additionally the high cost of litigation, wide ranging corruptions in the society in general, procedural difficulties in the access to justice have made it quite difficult for the peasant workers in ship breaking industry to rip the benefit of law that are available to them.

X. Conclusion

It has been observed from the discussion above that despite availability of numerous legal weaponries the temporary nature of job in shipbreaking industry in Bangladesh and serious lack of collecting bargaining for workers *inter alia* have resulted into a frustration in receiving the benefit of law. Controversies exist about the hazardous nature of EOL ships. The hazardous waste rule governing the hazardous industry in Bangladesh appears to have made an exception for EOL ships contrary to the Basel Convention of which Bangladesh is a party. Evidently, the shipbreaking regime appears to be more flexible than other hazardous waste regimes in Bangladesh that are still subject to the stricter jurisdiction under the Basel Convention. Considerable lack of coordination in enforcement mechanism has been observed. The provision on violation of the legal provisions of SBRR 2011 and BSRA 2018 and the sanction for violation do not reflect many realities on the ground and quite inefficient to demonstrate any retributive or compensatory effect.[273] Keeping all these fundamental issues outstanding, the framework regulations of Bangladesh on ship recycling seem to have contributed too little too late to ensure a safe, environmentally sound ship recycling industry in this preeminent ship recycling state.

Bangladesh along with other South Asian players has been in the premier positions in ship-breaking business for last three decades but there has been a recent change in the dynamics of global ship recycling industry. Shipowners are increasingly preferring green yards in China and

[272]Ishtiaque Ahmed, *'Unravelling Socio-economic and Ecological Distribution Conflicts in Ship Breaking in Bangladesh for Addressing Negative Externalities in Law and Policy Making'* Minnesota Journal Of International Law (Minn. J. Int. Law), 168-169 (2020), University of Minnesota Law School, USA.

[273]Ishtiaque Ahmed & Archana Reddy, SENSREC Project Phase II (Capacity Building) On file with author

Turkey.[274] On the other hand, India, which is the closest competitor to Bangladesh in global ship breaking has already acceded to the HKC recently in 2019.[275] There are currently about 45 ship recycling yards in India that have already obtained the statement of compliance with the HKC from international classification societies and more 15 ship breaking yards are now approaching towards this certification.[276] Almost 50% of the active recycling facilities in India have achieved the standards set by the HKC and its guidelines which no doubt will have a positive impact in India's competitiveness in this global business. Although it's not necessary for Bangladesh to ratify the HKC to apply its standards in its state territory, with the current circumstances as described, Bangladesh does not have many options in hand. If the gaps and the general inadequacies that have been identified in this article are not addressed by the government of Bangladesh within a reasonable time and if the power dynamics, politics and lobby cannot convince the recyclers in Bangladesh to avoid maneuvering the existing regulatory processes through undue exercise of their market powers, it may not be possible for Bangladesh to keep control and sustain the business in the long run.

---

[274]Sara Costa and Geetanjoy Sahu , The Ship Recycling Industry Must Move Towards a Sustainable Future, The Wire , 13 Aug 2020 www.thewire.in/environment/shipbreaking-ship-recycling-industry-sustainable-future-environment>

[275]International Shipping News, 'India Ratifies the Hong Kong International Convention for Safe and Environmentally Sound Recycling of Ships', Hellenic Shipping News, 22 Nov, 2019, www.hellenicshippingnews.com/india-ratifies-the-hong-kong-international-convention-for-safe-and-environmentally-sound-recycling-of-ships-2009/>

[276]Sam Chamber, PHP becomes first recycling yard in Bangladesh to become Hong Kong compliant, 24 Oct 2017 www.splash247.com/first-bangladesh-recycling-yard-becomes-hong-kong-compliant/>

Tourism Levy in Bali: Why Should Foreigners Be Charged Extra Fees?

I Made Budi Arsika[1]
International Law Department, Faculty of Law Udayana University, Bali-Indonesia

Ni Gusti Ayu Dyah Satyawati
Administrative Law Department, Faculty of Law Udayana University, Bali-Indonesia

I Nyoman Sirtha
Law and Society Department, Faculty of Law Udayana University, Bali-Indonesia

---

Summary. For years, the imposition of monetary contributions by foreign tourists in Bali has been a subject of debates and controversy. The rationale of foreign tourist contributions is that they facilitate the preservation of Bali's natural and cultural heritage. The recent enactment of the Bali Provincal Regulation No. 1 Year 2020 concerning Tourist Contributions for the Protection of the Natural Environment and Culture of Bali (the Provincial Regulation) seemingly solves the issue. However, a closer look suggests that the Provincial Regulation lacks a convincing legal concept of voluntary tourist contributions. This paper analyses the content, process, and expectation of the creation of the above-mentioned Provincial Regulation, with reference to Indonesian laws and regulations, and reports conclusions drawn from meetings and interviews with relevant authorities. It is argued that, instead of providing specific regulations of the collection and management of voluntary contributions, the Provincial Regulation delegates the Governor to determine these matters through executive order. Undoubtedly, this

[1]Corresponding author: budi_arsika@unud.ac.id

dissociates with stakeholder expectations related to the preservation of Bali's natural and cultural riches and the improvement of tourist facilities and services in Bali. Finally, the paper addresses the issue of implementing the Regulation in the light of the impact of the Covid-19 pandemic on tourism.

Keywords: Tourism levy; Voluntary contributions; Funding; Bali

Introduction

Bali is a province in the Unitary State of the Republic of Indonesia. Known worldwide as a tourist destination, Bali is divided into eight regencies (Badung, Bangli, Buleleng, Gianyar, Jembrana, Karangasem, Klungkung, and Tabanan) and a Municipality of Denpasar.

Bali develops cultural-based tourism, ensouled by Hinduism and the life philosophy of *Tri Hita Karana*.[2] Bali's unique cultural heritage has been recognized by the World Heritage Committee which inscribed the Cultural Landscape of Bali Province on the World Heritage List.[3] It expects the proper interconnection between culture and tourism in order to provide propriety to the society, culture, as well as the environment.[4]

Tourism is the biggest industry in Bali: for decades, the tourism sector has been contributing significantly to the Province's economy. The Global Destination Cities Index 2019 revealed that Bali is visited by 8,23 million foreign visitors each year, with an average stay of 8,6 days and daily spending of 125 American Dollars (henceforth, USD). The index also indicates that Bali is the world's highest tourist area that creates em-

[2]It is repeatedly enshrined in Bali Provincial Regulation No. 2 Year 2012 concerning Culture Tourism of Bali that replaced Bali Provincial Regulation No. 3 Year 1991 concerning Culture Tourism. The definition of culture tourism of Bali refers to Article 1(14) of Bali Provincial Regulation No. 2 Year 2012 concerning Culture Tourism of Bali.

[3]Decision Adopted by the World Heritage Committee No. 36 COM 8B.26, At Its 36th Session (Saint-Petersburg/ 2012), the Cultural Landscape of Bali Province: the Subak System as a Manifestation of the Tri Hita Karana Philosophy, Indonesia.

[4]Trimurti, C. P & Utama, I.G.B.R. (2019). Confirmation of the Tourism Marketing Mix Model in the Perspective of Foreign Tourists. *The International Journal of Business Management and Technology, 3(6)*, p.241.

ployment as it is estimated that 1,000 additional tourists support 409 jobs.[5]

In the context of financial administration, tourism does not directly correspond to the revenue of the Bali Provincial Government. Visa fees imposed on foreigners, including the 30-day Visa on Arrival (VoA) paid upon arrival at the Bali International Airport, are transferred to the Indonesian national government and are categorized as a non-tax revenue.[6] It is estimated that Bali Province contributes foreign exchange from cultural tourism amounting to 9-10,4 billion USD per year.[7] Bali Provincial Government, however, does not receive direct revenue from the national government for the rise in tourism foreign exchange.[8] The national law determines that profit-sharing funds can only be shared from natural resource revenues (such as forestry, general mining, fishery, petroleum mining, natural gas mining, and geothermal mining)[9], which are not sectors exploited in Bali. It has been argued for the necessity to submit a judicial review before the Constitutional Court of the Republic of Indonesia to examine whether or not the National Law on Fiscal Balance Between the National Government and Regional Government is contrary to the 1945 Constitution of the Republic of Indonesia.[10] The idea is to enable Bali to receive a proper sharing budget from the national govern-

---

[5]Mastercard. (2019). *Global Destination Cities Index 2019.* www.newsroom.mastercard.com/wp-content/uploads/2019/09/GDCI-Global-Report-FINAL-1.pdf (Accessed 19 January 2020).

[6]Article 9 of the Regulation of the Government of Republic of Indonesia No. 28 Year 2019 concerning Type and Tarif of Non-Tax Revenue Applies for Ministry of Law and Human Rights.

[7]Bali Puspa News. (2019). Senator Pastika Usulkan Ubah Nama Kontribusi menjadi Donasi pada Ranperda Kontribusi Wisatawan. www.www.balipuspanews.com/senator-pastika-usulkan-ubah-nama-kontribusi-menjadi-donasi-pada-ranperda-kontribusi-wisatawan.html (accessed 29 December 2019).

[8]The national government distributes its State budget to provincial and regency/municipality governments in Bali through various schemes that are not exclusively aimed at a return to the tourism activities in Bali.

[9]Article 11 (3) of the Law of the Republic of Indonesia No. 33 Year 2004 concerning Fiscal Balance Between the National Government and Regional Government.

[10]The power and competence of the Constitutional Court of the Republic of Indonesia in reviewing a Law (a type of national legislation that jointly adopted by the House of Representatives and the President) against the Constitution is stipulated in Article 24C (1) of the 1945 Constitution of the Republic of Indonesia

ment due to Bali's very large contribution in donating foreign exchange to the national government from tourism. [11]

The limited budget to preserve Bali's nature and culture might lead to ideas of exploiting nature and culture as tourism economic resources.[12]In the context of regional tax distribution, tourism-related taxes (e.g., hotel, restaurant, and entertainment, respectively) are in favour of regency and municipality governments, not the provincial government.[13] The province tax only comprises of motor vehicle tax, motor vehicle ownership change fee, motor vehicle gasoline tax, surface water fee, and cigarette tax.[14] As stated by Bali Province Governor, motor vehicle tax and motor vehicle ownership change fees are no longer subjected to increase due to the rising number of motor vehicles, resulting in an increase in traffic congestion and air pollution.[15]

This may be the main reason why Bali Province is lacking the budget to overcome the negative impacts of tourism. A study found that provincial and regency/municipality budgets allocated to preserve Bali's natural and cultural environment are insufficient compared to their increasing damages.[16] For example, agricultural lands were continuously converted to an average of 700 hectares per year,[17] mainly for the sake of constructing tourism accommodation. Undeniably, this would endanger self-production and local food businesses. In addition, Balinese culture

[11]Tribun Bali. (2019). DPD RI Perjuangkan 3 UU Untuk Bali: Pastika Sebut Provinsi Tak Dapat Apa-Apa Dari Pariwisata. www.bali.tribunnews.com/2019/12/07/dpd-ri-perjuangkan-3-uu-untuk-bali-pastika-sebut-provinsi-tak-dapat-apa-apa-dari-pariwisata (Accessed 29 December 2019).

[12]As an example, the idea of making culture as a tourism economic resource can be read in See Salain, M.S.P.D, Isles, D. & Wairocana, I.G.N. (2017). Regulating Indigenous Culture as a Tourism Economic Resource. Udayana Journal of Law and Culture, 1(2), p.133.

[13]Article 2 (2) of the Law of the Republic of Indonesia No. 28 Year 2009 concerning Regional Tax and Retribution

[14]Article 2 (1) of the Law of the Republic of Indonesia No. 28 Year 2009 concerning Regional Tax and Retribution

[15]Tribun Bali. (2019). Gubernur Koster Berupaya Cari Skema Baru Genjot PAD Bali.
www.bali.tribunnews.com/2019/10/31/gubernur-koster-berupaya-cari-skema-baru-genjot-pad-bali (Accessed 24 May 2020).

[16]Wiranatha, A.S, Pujaastawa, I.B.G., Antara, M. & Ariana, N. (2015). *Membangun Mekanisme Pendanaan Berkelanjutan Untuk Pelestarian Alam dan Budaya Bali*. Pusat Penelitian Kebudayaan dan Kepariwisataan and Conservation International Indonesia. Bali, p. 71.

[17]Bali Post. (2020). Alih Fungsi Lahan Pertanian di Bali Rata-Rata 700 Hektar per Tahun. http://www.balipost.com/news/2020/01/17/99216/Alih-Fungsi-Lahan-Pertanian-di...html

has been degrading as a result of globalisation, modernisation and tourism development.[18]

In 2018, the imposition of contributions of 10 USD per foreign tourist was introduced, and domestic tourists visiting Bali were required to pay 0.7 USD per visit. Such effort aimed to explore regional income, expecting that the Bali Provincial Government will be able to reach around 70 million USD per year, by assuming the number of tourist visits reaches 7 million people.[19] It was conceived that the fund should be used for the preservation of Bali's natural and cultural environment.[20] This led to the public assumption that such contributions are mandatory for foreign visitors, compensating for the impact of tourism on nature and culture preservation. This Governor's idea seems to support the concept of making Bali as a 'one island tourism management system', in which the money collected at the provincial level are to be distributed to regencies and muncipality in supporting their cultural, environmental, and infrastructure needs.[21] This initiative is promising, as the fund may be usedfor cultural preservation[22] and tourism programs[23] in the regions.

This Governor's idea received both support and disagreement by tourism stakeholders. For example, the Chairman of the Indonesian Hotel and *Restaurant* Association of the Badung Regency supported the idea and sought alternative means of collecting tourism contributions, including airport service charges when travelers enter Bali or a combination

---

[18](Accessed 19 January 2020).
Bali Travel News. (2016). Budaya Bali Alami Degradasi. http://bali-travelnews.com/2016/12/28/budaya-bali-alami-degradasi/ (Accessed 19 January 2020).

[19]Nusa Bali. (2018). Bali Bidik PAD Rp 1 Trilyun dari Turis. www.www.nusabali.com/berita/41956/bali-bidik-pad-rp-1-triliun-dari-turis

[20]Tribun Bali. (2018). Gubernur Bali Wacanakan Biaya Kontribusi Masuk ke Bali Turis Asing Bayar 10 Dolar lokal Rp 10 ribu. www.travel.tribunnews.com/2018/11/20/gubernur-bali-wacanakan-biaya-kontribusi-masuk-ke-bali-turis-asing-bayar-10-dolar-lokal-rp-10-ribu (Accessed 17 March 2019).

[21]This concept was explained by Nurjaya, I G. (Secretary of Nayaka -Expert team of the Customary Village Assembly/Majelis Desa Adat/MDA of the Bali Province). Interview held in Denpasar, 16 October 2019.

[22]Supanji, I G.N. and Sumerta, I M.G. (Head and Secretary Tabanan Regency Culture Office). Interview held in Tabanan, 4 September 2019.

[23]Sukadewi, N. K. M. (Head of the Tourism Destination Division of the Regional Tourism Office of Gianyar Regency). Interview held in Gianyar, 30 July 2019.

between airline ticket and airport tax.[24] A General Manager of airports in Indonesia was in an opinion that the levy through airline tickets should be reduced into only 5 USD.[25] On the contrary, the Chairperson of the Indonesian Tourism Intellectual Association expressed his disagreement with the plan because it would reduce tourist arrivals to Bali by 15 percent.[26]

Strong objections were also expressed by the International Air Transport Association (IATA) in relation to the method of collection, including the levy in the airline tickets.[27] In January 2019, the IATA Regional Vice President for the Asia Pacific warned the Government of Bali that the initiative contravenes to the International Civil Aviation Organization (ICAO)'s taxation policy.[28] He refers to Article 15 of the Convention on International Civil Aviation (Chicago Convention) that regulates "*No fees, dues or other charges shall be imposed by any contracting State in respect solely of the right of transit over or entry into or exit from its territory of any aircraft of a contracting State or persons or property thereon*". Indonesia ratified the Convention since 27 April 1950,[29] which entails that it has an international legal obligation to respect and implement the provisions contained in the convention.

The Indonesian Minister of Tourism, in responding to this proposal, states that levies should be packaged creatively. Additionally, local lead-

---

[24]Tribun Bali. (2019). PHRI Optimis Wisman Tak Surut ke Bali: Rencana Retribusi 10 dolar per Wisatawan. www.bali.tribunnews.com/2019/07/16/rencana-retribusi-10-dolar-per-wisatawan-phri-optimistis-wisman-tak-surut-ke-bali (accessed 31 August 2019).

[25]Nusa Bali. (2019). AP I Minta Pungutan Turis Cukup 5 Dolar. www.www.nusabali.com/berita/45662/ap-i-minta-pungutan-turis-cukup-5-dolar (accessed 31 August 2019)

[26]Ekonomi Bisnis. (2019). Wisman ke Bali Bakal Dikenai Pungutan US 10 Pelaku Pariwisata Protes. www.ekonomi.bisnis.com/read/20190121/12/880827/wisman-ke-bali-bakal-dikenai-pungutan-us10-pelaku-pariwisata-protes (accessed 31 August 2019).

[27]Antara News. (2019). Koster: Biaya kontribusi wisatawan disatukan dengan tiket pesawat. www.bali.antaranews.com/berita/135334/koster-biaya-kontribusi-wisatawan-disatukan-dengan-tiket-pesawat (accessed 31 August 2019).

[28]The Jakarta Post. (2019). Global Airline Group IATA Objects to Planned Bali Tourist Tax. www.www.thejakartapost.com/news/2019/02/19/global-airline-group-iata-objects-to-planned-bali-tourist-tax.html (accessed 31 August 2019).

[29]ICAO. Convention on International Civil Aviation Signed at Chicago on 7 December 1944 (List of Signatories). www.www.icao.int/secretariat/legal/List%20of%20Parties/Chicago_EN.pdf
(accessed 29 December 2019).

ers should think of the possibility of elasticity in marketing, in which, if costs increase, the level of visits will decrease.[30]

In spite of raised criticism and objections, the Bali Regional House of Representatives and Bali Province Governor jointly approved the Draft of Bali Provincial Regulation concerning Protection of Bali's Natural Environment and Culture through Tourism Contributions (hereinafter, the Draft) in August 2019.[31] At that time, the draft was becoming a contending document that would determine whether or not the levy on tourists is legitimate. Despite political optimism, the efforts were shadowed by unsuccessful stories in the past. For example, in 2013 the Bali Province Governor issued a regulation imposing a mandatory levy to foreign tourists 10 USD, in which 5 USD will be donated to culture and environment preservation and 5 USD will be used as safety insurance for foreign tourists during their stay on Bali.[32] During this period, the regulation could not be implemented as it was considered incompatible with the Law of the Republic of Indonesia, No. 28 Year 2009 concerning the Regional Tax and Regional Retribution.[33]

After a series of consultations and facilitations, the Bali Provincal Regulation No. 1 Year 2020 concerning Tourist Contributions for the Protection of the Natural Environment and Culture of Bali (hereinafter, the Provincial Regulation) was officially enacted in April 2020.[34] The final version modified and inserted some contents provided in the Draft by, among others, slightly adjusting the title, emphasising the voluntary character of the contribution, and detailing supervision and monitoring apparatus. This provincial regulation seems to be a remarkable achieve-

---

[30]Bali Travel News. (2018) Rencana Pungutan 10 Dolar per Wisatawan Mesti Dikemas dengan Kreatif. www.bali-travelnews.com/2018/09/25/rencana-pungutan-10-dolar-per-wisatawan-mesti-dikemas-dengan-kreatif/ (Accessed 24 May 2020)

[31]Antara News. (2019). DPRD Bali Beri Saran untuk Ranperda Kontribusi Wisatawan. www.bali.antaranews.com/berita/158938/dprd-bali-beri-saran-untuk-ranperda-kontribusi-wisatawan
(accessed 29 December 2019).

[32]Regulation of Bali Province Governor No 41 Year 2013 concerning the Amendment of Regulation of Bali Province Governor No 58 Year 2012 concerning Programs of Culture Preservation and Environmental Protection

[33]Agung Suryawan Wiranatha, et.al, Membangun Mekanisme Pendanaan Berkelanjutan Untuk Pelestarian Alam dan Budaya Bali, Result of Research, Pusat Penelitian Kebudayaan dan Kepariwisataan Universitas Udayana and Conservation International Indonesia, Bali, 2015, p. 58-59.

[34]Jaringan Dokumentasi dan Informasi Hukum PEmerintah Provinsi Bali. (2020). Perda No.1 Tahun 2020. www.jdih.baliprov.go.id/produk-hukum/peraturan-perundang-undangan/perda/28547 (accessed 14 June 2020).

ment, compared to the other proposals that have never been realized for decades.[35]

The present analysis focuses on the content of the Provincial Regulation, its process, and the expected outcome following its implementation. For the purposes of this paper, the monetary sums will be presented in US dollars (at the rate, USD1 = IDR 14,400).[36] The paper primarily analyses relevant legal instruments, mainly Indonesian law and regulations. Opinion, perception, and clarification were gained from interviewees through qualitative interviews and open discussion. The interviewees are a senator at the national level, government officials at provincial and regency/municipality levels, Secretary of expert team of Bali's Customary Village Assembly, and lawyer. This legal research may be useful for interdisciplinary readers as it covers economic, tourism, and cultural perspectives in the analysis. The paper also offers a perspective to legal scholars, decision-makers, and tourism stakeholders especially regarding the creation of regulations and policies in the field of tourism. Besides, it may become a lesson learned reference to those involved in the tourism taxation/levy and management of regional tourism destinations. Finally, it is important to mention that, given the lack of scholarly work on tourism levy in Bali, some of the resources here come from online newspaper articles that address this issue. Therefore, this paper provides new knowledge and opportunities for future research on the legislation related to tourism taxation/levy in Bali.

The Global Context of Tourism Taxes: Lesson Learned for Bali

The term 'tourist contribution' and 'tourism levy' used in this paper are relatively parallel to the meaning of 'tourism tax' which is generally used

[35]Gede Nurjaya reveals that, as far as he remember, the idea of an integrated and centralized levy for tourists in the Province of Bali has ever been discussed in the mid of 90-s at the level of Chairmen of Tourism Offices in Bali until the recent years. During this period, tourism officials faced various obstacles as well as non-unanimous commitment from regencies and city in Bali. Therefore, he appreciate the works of the current provincial administration. Nurjaya, I G. (Secretary of *Nayaka* -Expert team of the Customary Village Assembly/*Majelis Desa Adat*/MDA of the Bali Province). Interview held in Denpasar, 16 October 2019.

[36]It based on assumption of currency exchange, as appears in Elucidation of Law of the Republic of Indonesia No.20 Year 2019 concerning State Budget Revenues and Expenditures of the Year 2020, dated 18 October 2019. para 1.

in global tourism. On the issue 'taxation and tourism', taxes are described as:

> compulsory unrequited payments to general government – including the central administration, agencies whose operations are under its effective control, state and local governments and their administrations, certain social security schemes and autonomous government entities, excluding public enterprises.[37]

The United Nations World Tourism Organization (UNWTO) defines tourism taxes as

> …taxes... applicable specifically to tourists and the tourism sector or, alternatively, if not specific to the tourism sector, those which are applied differently in tourist destinations.[38]

In basic terms, UNWTO underlines that tourist taxes should be harmonized between countries and regions to minimise competitive distortions between destinations.[39] The UNWTO has been consistent in advising countries to be wise in issuing tax policies for tourists. As an example, in May 2014, the UNWTO Secretary-General, Taleb Rifai, urged African countries to consider the taxation of air passengers and hotel guests and its possible consequences on tourism demand, economic growth and jobs in the tourism sector in Africa.[40] The UNWTO Global Code of Ethics for Tourism (GCET)[41] also guides that "*specific taxes and levies penalizing the tourism industry and undermining its competitiveness should be gradually phased out or corrected.*" [42]

The practice of countries and regions also indicates the variety in imposing tourism tax and levy.

---

[37]OECD. (2014). *OECD Tourism Trends and Policies 2014*. OECD Publishing. Paris. p. 75.

[38]Ihalanayake, R. (2007). *Economics of Tourism Taxation: A Study of Tourism Taxes in Australia*, A thesis submitted in total fulfilment of the requirements for the degree of Doctor of Philosophy, School of Applied Economics, Faculty of Business and Law, Victoria University, Melbourne, p. 13.

[39]UNWTO. (2011) *Policy and Practice for Global Tourism*, United Nations World Tourism Organization. Madrid, p. 102.

[40]UNWTO. (2014). *UNWTO* Cautions against Potential Tourism Tax in Africa. Press Release No: PR14033, 13 May 2014.

[41]Resolution adopted by the General Assembly 21 December 2001 A/RES/56/212 Global Code of Ethics for Tourism.

[42]Article 8 (4) of the UNWTO Global Code of Ethics for Tourism.

Austria is an example of a country that applies a variety of general and tourism-specific taxes, including corporate and personal income, real estate, VAT, occupancy, and air passenger duty/departure taxes.[43] In January 2019, Japan adopted a scheme of tourist tax that was nicknamed as “sayonara tax.” The tax targetted visitors leaving Japan by airplane and port to pay a 1,000 yen (10 USD). The money will be utilized to diversify and build up infrastructures for tourists.[44]

The imposition of sustainable tourism tax which is intended as a contribution to environmental conservation has been practiced by the Balearic Government to almost all Mallorca visitors. This tax is applied to hotels, villas, and cruise ships. Similar taxation policies have also been applied in France, Germany, Italy, and Croatia.[45]

There are some studies on the practice of levy in the regions conducted by local authorities. For instance, a study by Li, Guo, Zhu and Chen (2010) proposes that all tourists in the environmental conservation in Miyun County, Peoples’ Republic of China to become taxpayers of 5% - 15% of their total expenses during the visit which is collected through the entrance of tourist attractions objects and other forms. Li et al. argue that a high quality of ecology may fall into the scope of a public product. Therefore, the government may impose a tax on tourists that will be utilized for the conservation and advancement of the environment.[46]

Instead of an increasing tax, some researches indicate that reducing tourism-related tax is an effective means of supporting the countries’ macroeconomics, especially in the investment sector. In Albania, the decreasing of tourism value-added tax (VAT) from 20% to 6% will attract public, private, domestic and foreign investment; increase income derived from foreign nationals and tour operators; and will lead to the formalisation of the economy and especially to the tourism sector.[47] In Jor-

---

[43]PricewaterhouseCoopers LLP-Europena Commission. (2017). *The Impact of Taxes on the Competitiveness of European Tourism*, Final Report. Luxembourg: Publications Office of the European Union, p. 178-180.

[44]Independent. (2019). Japan Tourist Tax Cost Levy Airport Tourism Tokyo Olympics 2020. www.www.independent.co.uk/travel/news-and-advice/japan-tourist-tax-cost-levy-airport-tourism-tokyo-olympics-2020-a8721451.html (accessed 29 December 2019).

[45]ABC Mallorca. (2019). What is Mallorca’s tourist tax? www.www.abc-mallorca.com/balearic-tourist-tax-doubles/ (accessed 31 August 2019).

[46]Li, Y., Guo, L., Zhu, W. and Chen, F. (2010). Feasibility Analysis of Collecting Environmental Protection Tax from Tourist in an Environmental Concervation Area: A Case Study of Miyun County, in C. A. Brebbia and F. D. Pineda (Ed), *Sustainable Tourism IV*. WIT Press. Southampton. p. 280-281.

[47]Cela, G. (2018). The Impact Assessment of the VAT Reduction in Tourism Sector. *European Scientific Journal, 14 (25)*, p. 243, 253.

dan, a 2% reduction of tax applies to tourism accommodation rooms successfully elevated their occupancy rates and attracted more foreign direct investment into the country.[48]

A comparative study on Italian and Russian tourist tax found that the revenues are intended to support cultural and environmental heritage, tourist infrastructure, and public services. However, the imposition of a tourist tax in both countries has been severely criticized by the association of hoteliers as the non-residents deemed unfair to pay for services that are not enjoyed.[49]

Furthermore, in Zanzibar, where tourism becomes the largest source of foreign exchange, the tax system led to an extensive administrative burden. This is in line with the abstention of a particular law that is designed for tour operators, restaurants, and hotels levies.[50]

What Bali should learn from the global framework and practice on tourism tax, with regards to the creation of Provincial Regulation? The reasons behind the creation of this regulation are similar to existing practices in some countries, e.g., sustainable tourism tax for environmental conservation by the Balearic Government as well as tourism tax in Italia and Russia that was intended to support cultural and environmental heritage. This, hence, makes clear that the Bali government's idea is not something brand new in a global tourism practice, and should not be regarded as a controversial concept. However, the Bali Provincial Government should pay attention to the threat of competitiveness arising from the imposition of tourism levy. Besides, there is a need to define taxpayers, the percentage, and the procedures to prevent complexity and uncertainty in the levy system.

FINANCIAL CAPACITY OF BALI PROVINCE

In order to assess whether or not Bali Province really needs the tourism levy, it is necessary to look at its financial capacity. As part of the Unitary State of the Republic of Indonesia, the Bali Province Government has to comply with existing national laws and regulations in the field of

---

[48]Falade Obalade, T.A. & Dubey, S. (2014). Managing Tourism as a Source of Revenue and Foreign Direct Investment Inflow in a Developing Country: The Jordanian Experience. International Journal of Academic Research in Economics and Management *Sciences, 3(3),* p. 30.

[49]Fontana, C. & Lagutin, I. (2018). Tourist Taxes in Italy and Russia. *Russian Law Journal, VI(1),* p.87, 88, 97.

[50]Mahangila, D. & Anderson, W. (2017). Tax Administrative Burdens in the Tourism Sector in Zanzibar: Stakeholders' Perspectives, *SAGE Open,* p. 1, 11, 12.

regional finance, especially those related to the delegation of some authorities by the national government to the regions. Article 285 paragraph (1) of the Law of the Republic of Indonesia No. 23 of 2014 concerning Local Government (Local Government Law) that determines the sources of regional revenue are consists of:

1. Locally-generated revenue (Regional original income) which includes regional taxes; regional retribution (levy); results of the management of separated regional assets; and other legitimate locally-generated revenue;
2. Transfer revenue; and
3. Other legitimate regional revenue.

Below is a description of how the provisions on regional revenue as stipulated in the Local Government Law is implemented by the Bali Province in the Year 2019.

Regional Revenue (total A+B+C)				**439,131,841**
A	**Locally-Generated Revenue (a1 + a2 + a3 + a4)**		**249,145,779**	
	a1. Regional tax	213,141,418		
	a2. Regional retribution	3,458,575		
	a3. Results of the management of separated regional assets	11,864,971		
	a4. Other legitimate locally-generated revenue	20,678,731		
B.	**Balance fund (b1 + b2 + b3)**		**184,862,978**	
	b1. Tax revenue sharing / non-tax revenue sharing	12,916,251		
	b2. General allocation fund	92,072,747		
	b3. special allocation fund	79,874		

C	**Other legitimate regional income (c1 + c2 + c3 +c4 + c5)**		**5,123,083**
	c1. Grants	370,694	
	c2. Emergency fund	0	
	c3. Tax revenue sharing	0	
	c4. Adjustment and special autonomy funds	4,752.389	
	c5. Financial assistance from the province or from other local governments	0	

Table 1 Details of Regional Revenue of Bali Province Year 2019 (in American dollars: 1 USD equal to 14,400 IDR)[51]

As can be seen, the total regional revenue of the Bali Province in 2019 is 439,131,841 USD. More than fifty percent of its total revenue is collected from locally-generated revenue, primarily regional tax sourced from motor vehicle tax. This regional revenue should be compared with other elements, including the number of population and the Gross Regional Domestic Product (GDP) per capita. In 2018, the projected total population of Bali is amounted to 4.29 million people, while the GDP per capita based on applicable/current prices (*atas dasar harga berlaku / adhb*) reached 3,793 USD.[52]

There is increased revenue in 2020 compared to the previous year. The total regional revenue in 2020 is 458,717,525 USD, consisting of locally-generated revenue (261,282,979 USD); Balance fund (193,529,209 USD); and Other legitimate regional income (3,905,336 USD).[53] Both locally-generated revenue and balance fund components are increased

[51]Source: Articles 1 and 2 of the Bali Provincial Regulation No. 10 Year 2018 concerning Regional Budget Revenues and Expenditures Semesta Berencana of the Year 2019.

[52]Badan Pusat Statistik Provinsi Bali (2019). Pertumbuhan Ekonomi Bali Tahun 2018. www.bali.bps.go.id/pressrelease/2019/02/06/717261/pertumbuhan-ekonomi-bali--tahun-2018.html (Accessed 29 December 2019).

[53]Articles 1 and 2 of the Bali Provincial Regulation No. 11 Year 2019 concerning Regional Budget Revenues and Expenditures *Semesta Berencana* of the Year 2020

while the decreasing only on the component of other legitimate regional income.

At a glance, Bali Province seems to have a strong financial capacity in the context of Indonesia as a developing country, considering that Bali itself does not have natural resources to be exploited in the big-scale mining industry. One should take into account that Bali Provincial budgets allocated to preserve Bali's natural and cultural environment are insufficient, compared to their increasing damages.[54] It has been an annual practice that Bali Provincial Government allocates special financial assistance in its regional budget to support customary village, traditional water irrigation system (*subak*), means of ceremonies, built places of worship, the activities of arts groups, as well as organises annual Bali Arts Festival.[55] There is indeed an extra income to fund those needs.

The Content of the Provincial Regulation

The national law determines that regional taxes and levies are stipulated by Law and to make it effective in the regions, it will be further regulated by the Regional Regulations.[56] The national The provision also confirms that the Regional Government is prohibited from making levies or other designations exclude those stipulated in the law which, among others, causes a high-cost economy and hamper the mobility of the population.[57]

The above framework seems was realized by the Bali Province Government when initiating the Draft of Provincial Regulation concerning Protection of Bali's Natural Environment and Culture through Tourism Contributions (hereinafter, 'the draft').

In the context of the hierarchy of law, the Provincial Regulation refers to some national laws and regulations *inter alia* Law No. 10 Year 2009 concerning Tourism, Law No. 32 Year 2009 concerning Environmental

[54]Wiranatha, A.S, Pujaastawa, I.B.G., Antara, M. & Ariana, N.(2015). *Membangun Mekanisme Pendanaan Berkelanjutan Untuk Pelestarian Alam dan Budaya Bali*. Pusat Penelitian Kebudayaan dan Kepariwisataan and Conservation International Indonesia. Bali, p. 71.

[55]Bali Puspa News. (2019). Senator Pastika Usulkan Ubah Nama Kontribusi menjadi Donasi pada Ranperda Kontribusi Wisatawan. www.www.balipuspanews.com/senator-pastika-usulkan-ubah-nama-kontribusi-menjadi-donasi-pada-ranperda-kontribusi-wisatawan.html (accessed 29 December 2019).

[56]Article 286 (1) of the Law No. 23 Year 2014 concerning Local Government

[57]Article 286 (2) of the Law No. 23 Year 2014 concerning Local Government and Article 32 of the Government Regulation No. 12 Year 2019 concerning Regional Financial Management.

Protection and Management, Law No. 23 Year 2014 concerning Local Government, Law No. 5 Year 2017 concerning Advancement of Culture, Government Regulation No. 27 of 2014 concerning Management of State / Regional Property and Government Regulation No. 12 Year 2019 concerning Regional Financial Management. It is quite clear that the Provincial Regulation does not refer to the national law and regulation on taxation and retribution, considering that this proposed contribution scheme does not fit into those legal regimes.

The Provincial Regulation uses the term 'contribution' rather than 'tax, 'retribution', or 'levy.' There was also an idea to replace the term 'contribution' with 'donation', by considering that the latest term, in the legal sense, is not similar to either regional tax or regional retribution that are strictly regulated under the national law.[58] In a very normative legal sense, defining a legal term will determine the scope and applicability of a law or regulation. Choosing a correct legal term, in the context of Bali Province interests, may become a breakthrough in hindering strict applicability of laws on taxation and retribution.

Article 3 of the Provincial Regulation mentions six purposes to arrange the tourist contribution, namely:

1. protection of nature and environment and waste management;
2. protection of customs, traditions, arts and culture, and local wisdom;
3. accelerating and strengthening efforts to advance Balinese culture as part of national culture by upholding the spirit of unity in diversity;
4. empowerment of customary village;
5. construction of arts and cultural facilities and infrastructure; and
6. improvement of the quality of service and organization of tourism in Bali.

Almost all legal and political debates during the creating of this regulation are centered in Article 4 of the Provincial Regulation. Article 4 (1) of

[58]Statement by Made Mangku Pastika, a National Senator at the Regional Representative Council and the Former Governor of Bali. Radar Bali. (2019). Biar tak Masuk Unsur Pajak Pastika Usul Kata Donasi jadi Judul Perda. www.radarbali.jawapos.com/read/2019/12/15/170322/biar-tak-masuk-unsur-pajak-pastika-usul-kata-donasi-jadi-judul-perda (Accessed 29 December 2019). The statement was confirmed during the interview. Pastika, M.M. (National Senator at the Regional Representative Council, representing Bali Province). Interview held in Denpasar, 2nd January 2020.

the Provincial Regulation requires every tourist visiting the Bali Province to contribute to the protection of the nature and culture of Bali. The phrase 'every tourist' means both domestic and foreign tourists who travel to Bali.[59] It makes clear that this expected regulation does not exclusively target foreigners, but also Indonesian tourists as well.

Next, Article 4 (2) mentions that the tourist contribution is a voluntary contribution that can be donated in the form of goods and/or money. The voluntary contribution by tourists seems was adopted as a modest and realistic compromise to accommodate the political aspiration in legitimising the 'levy' on one hand but does not incompatible to the higher law and regulation that prohibits and restricts such type of levy. Therefore, the meaning of 'voluntary contribution' in this Provincial Regulation cannot be understood in a generic meaning of tourism taxes and levies that are practiced in various countries and regions in the world. Presumably, the voluntary contributions will not generate yearly profit of 70 million USD to Bali Provincial Government, as what has been expected in 2018.

Besides, Article 4 does not specify the means of collecting the contribution as it only determines that the contributions are facilitated/communicated to the tourists by the provincial apparatus that handles tourism affairs as evidenced by a receipt.

Subsequently, Article 5 explains that provisions regarding the management of tourist Contributions will be further regulated in the Governor Regulation. In addition, Article 6 of the draft assures tourists that they will get benefit from the imposition of contributions in the form of:

1. improvement of tourism information services that are comprehensive, integrated and up to date;
2. clean, beautiful and sustainable natural environment both in material and spiritual (*sekala* and *niskala*) aspects;
3. diverse of customs, traditions, arts and culture, and local wisdom as well as giving spiritual aura (*metaksu*);
4. cleanliness, orderliness, comfort, and safety in the area of tourist destinations;
5. service in the time of a disaster; and
6. service and organization of higher quality Bali tourism.

---

[59]Article 1 (1) of the Bali Provincal Regulation No .1 Year 2020 concerning Tourist Contributions for the Protection of the Natural Environment and Culture of Bali

The contents of Article 6 reflect the statement of Discussion Coordinator of the Draft of Provincial Regulation who emphasises that the imposition of tourist contributions must provide returns and benefits for tourists in the form of improving tourism information services that are comprehensive, integrated and up to date. Besides, it underlines the concerns on cleanliness, order, comfort, and security in the tourist destination area, acceleration of service in the event of a disaster, priority hospital services as well as service delivery of higher quality Bali tourism.[60] The promised benefits for tourists as stipulated in Article 6, are likely to be similar to those designated by other regions and countries, aiming to elevate the quality of tourism, in line with cultural and natural preservation efforts. Tourists who visit Bali are promised peculiar benefits such as enjoying the intangible spiritual experiences known as *niskala* and *taksu*. They serve as non-measurable benefits that may be a distinctive experience from other tourism destinations in the world. Article 7 of the Provincial Regulation determines that if tourists do not get the benefits referred to in Article 6, they can submit a written complaint to the Tourism Office apparatus, to be followed up in accordance with the provisions of the legislation.

Supervision and monitoring are essential matters that are covered in the Provincial Regulation. As determined in Article 8 of the Provincial Regulation, the Governor conducts supervision and monitoring for the implementation of Tourist Contributions. These functions technically carried out by the Regional Apparatus that handles the affairs of Tourism while tourist contributions in the form of goods and/or money carried out by the Government Internal Supervisory Apparatus.

In addition, Article 9 ensure that public may play a role in the implementation of this Provincial Regulation through providing of inputs and suggestions as well as supervision of the use of the Tourist Contribution funds.

The Process

Procedural matters raise after the Plenary Meeting of the Bali Regional House of Representatives on 20 August 2019 approved the Governor's

---

[60]Statement given during the Plenary Meeting of the Bali Regional House of Representatives that approved the governor's proposal to become a draft of provincial regulation, on 20 August 2019. Antara News. (2019). DPRD Bali Beri Saran untuk Ranperda Kontribusi Wisatawan. www.bali.antaranews.com/berita/158938/dprd-bali-beri-saran-untuk-ranperda-kontribusi-wisatawan (accessed 29 December 2019).

proposal to become a Draft of Provincial Regulation. The 'game' was then shifted to the national government. Basically, Article 18 of Law Number 10 Year 2009 concerning Tourism (Tourism Law) stipulates that Regional Governments may regulate and manage tourism affairs in accordance with statutory provisions, however, it does not explicitly authorize the provincial government to impose tourism tax and retribution.[61]

The national government seems to have a concern about the subsequent impact of this regulation. From a political approach to law, a potential impact is the demands from other provincial or regency/municipality governments in Indonesia to establish regional regulations that imposing a levy on tourists for similar reasons or slightly different arguments. Rational considerations may be focused on the issue whether such type of levy would effectively support the tourism, cultural and environmental aspects of the region or, in contrary, it would be counterproductive to the efforts of the national and regional governments in promoting foreign tourists to several priority tourism destinations in Indonesia.

As revealed by the Governor of Bali Province in August 2019, the Ministry of Finance was of the view that there are no laws and regulations that may be used as a basis for the establishment of such provincial regulations because it can not be categorized as regional tax or regional retribution as stipulated in Law No. 28 Year 2009 concerning Regional Tax and Regional Retribution.[62] Whatsoever, the Governor continuously aims to persuade the national government by arguing that Law No. 23 Year 2014 concerning Local Government basically permits local governments to explore other sources of income. The Governor acknowledges that, despite that the Ministry of Tourism and the Ministry of Domestic Affairs have agreed on this draft, it still needs to be synchronized with the Directorate General of Fiscal Balance, a national government

[61]Article 29 of Law of the Republic of Indonesia No. 10 Year 2009 concerning Tourism states that the Provincial Government is given the authority to implement the following matters: establish and determine a provincial tourism development master plan; coordinating the implementation of tourism in the region; registration of tourism business; determining provincial tourism destinations; establish provincial tourist attractions; facilitate the promotion of tourism destinations and tourism products in the region; maintain provincial assets that are the tourist attraction of the province; and allocate the tourism budget.

[62]Bali Express. (2019). Dewan Bali Sahkan Ranperda Perubahan RTRW dan Kontribusi Wisatawan. www.baliexpress.jawapos.com/read/2019/08/21/151775/dewan-bali-sahkan-ranperda-perubahan-rtrw-dan-kontribusi-wisatawan (Accessed 29 December 2019).

body under the Ministry of Finance. [63] The Directorate General has the authority to formulate and implement the policies regarding regional taxes and retributions and to establish the relevant norms, standards, procedures, and criteria in those two matters.[64] Hope arises when, on 11 November 2019, revealed that the draft is waiting for the results of facilitation from the Ministry of Home Affairs.[65]

On 6 December 2019, the Speakers of Bali House of Representatives informed the Senators of the Regional Representative Council regarding the stuck of the draft and requested support.[66] As a follow-up, the draft was then discussed by Senator Made Mangku Pastika, Officials of Bali Provincial Government Bureau of Law and Human Rights and some members of an expert team on 13 December 2019.[67] On the same day, the heads of the Bali Regional House of Representatives conveyed aspirations to the Ministry of Home Affairs in Jakarta, in which the Ministry supported the Draft. After a series of consultation and facilitation between regional and national governments, the Ministry of Home Affairs in January 2020 sending a letter that granting a registration number to the Draft,[68] The granting of registration number indicating that verification of the result of facilitation and the improved draft has already been done and that the draft can officially be stipulated as a Provincial Regulation by Governor to be further promulgated in the regional gazette.[69]

---

[63]Bali Express. (2019). Dewan Bali Sahkan Ranperda Perubahan RTRW dan Kontribusi Wisatawan. www.baliexpress.jawapos.com/read/ 2019/08/21/151775/dewan-bali-sahkan-ranperda-perubahan-rtrw-dan-kontribusi-wisatawan (Accessed 29 December 2019).

[64]Article 32 and 33 of the Regulation of the President of the Republic of Indonesia No. 28 Year 2015 concerning the Ministry of Finance.

[65]Bali Puspa News. (2019). Perkuat UMKM, Dewan Bali Dukung Pemprov Tambah Penyertaan Modal di BPD Bali. www.www.balipuspanews.com/ perkuat-umkm-dewan-bali-dukung-pemprov-tambah-penyertaan-modal-di-bpd-bali.html (Accessed 24 May 2020).

[66]Ngastawa, K. (Lawyer). Interview held in Denpasar, 14 January 2020.

[67]Antara News. (2019). Senator Pastika Ubah Nama Ranperda Kontribusi Wisatawan.
www.bali.antaranews.com/berita/173032/senator-pastika-ubah-nama-ranperda-kontribusi-wisatawan (Accessed 29 December 2019).

[68]Letter of Head of Legal Bureau of the Ministry of Home Affairs to the Head of Legal Bureau of Bali Province No.
188.341/02/NR/BHK, dated 14 January 2020.

[69]Articles 1 (23) and (31),101, 103 (1), 104 (1) of the Minister of Home Affairs Regulation No.80 Year 2015 concerning The Establishment of Regional Regulations, as latest amended by Minister of Home Affairs Regulation No.120 Year 2018.

Expecting The Upcoming Implementing Regulation

The implementing regulation of the Provincial Regulation regarding the management of tourists contribution is expected to be issued by the Governor at the latest six months after the enactment, that is in October 2020.[70] The upcoming Regulation of Bali Province Governor is expected to regulate more technical aspects.

The benefits related to the protection of Bali's natural and cultural environment outlined in the Provincial Regulation include waste management equipment, ambulance cars, plant seeds, cleaning equipment, traditional musical instruments, and others[71], while there is no explanation regarding the currency to be used for contribution in the form of money. The regulation also fails to explain in what form receipts will be made: as physical copies or online formats. Therefore, the upcoming Governor Regulation has to detail the flows of the contribution, the type of currency, and receipt.

Besides, the governor regulation should include the priority of environmental and cultural programs to be funded and the sharing of contribution to regencies and municipality in Bali as well as some relevant stakeholders in the fields of environment, culture, and tourism. Also, it should ensure the improvement of tourism facilities that can be directly enjoyed by tourists and industries as taxpayers.[72] As Bali is developing cultural tourism, the contributions may be used to advancing and fund the ten cultural aspects, namely:[73]

1. oral tradition;
2. manuscript;
3. customs;

[70]Article 5 and 10 of the Bali Provincal Regulation No .1 Year 2020 concerning Tourist Contributions for the Protection of the Natural Environment and Culture of Bali

[71]Elucidation of Article 4 (2) of the Bali Provincal Regulation No .1 Year 2020 concerning Tourist Contributions for the Protection of the Natural Environment and Culture of Bali

[72]A study argues that tourism tax would be more generally accepted by industry and tourists, if there was tangible evidence that a consistent proportion of its revenue was used to improve tourism facilities. See Pazienza, P. (2011). Should we tax tourism? Theoretical justifications from the economics of non-renewable resource use, *Environmental Economics, 2(1)*, p. 14.

[73]Negara, A.A.K.S. (Secretary of Culture Office Bali Province). Interview held in Denpasar, 15 October 2019.

4. rite (religious ceremony);
5. traditional knowledge;
6. traditional technology;
7. art;
8. language;
9. folk games;
10. traditional sports[74] .

Furthermore, the tourist contributions may be used to finance the cultural heritage[75] and strengthen the existence of customary villages in Bali.[76] It is in line with the policy of Bali Province in establishing the Office of Customary Village Advancement in October 2019 that is assigned to handling the matters related to 1,943 customary villages in Bali.[77] This year, each village has received a fund of 20,833 USD.[78] The tourist contributions, indeed, would have the potential to increase the fund for customary village activities in the future. For example, the contributions could be allocated to stimulate *Baga Utsaha Padruwen Desa Adat* [79] tin seeking creative and sustainable ways of combining cultural events/ceremonies and profitable tourism activities.

---

[74]The category of cultural advancing objects in accordance with Article 5 of the Law No. 5 Year 2017 concerning the Advancement of Culture.

[75]As stipulated in Law of the Republic of Indonesia No. 11 Year 2010 concerning Cultural Heritage.

[76]Negara, A.A.K.S. (Secretary of Culture Office Bali Province). Interview held in Denpasar, 15 October 2019.

[77]Article 3(1)(d) of the Bali Provincial Regulation No. 7 Year 2019 Concerning Amendment to Regional Regulation N0. 10 Year 2016 concerning Formation and Arrangement of Regional Organization.

[78]Antaranews. (2020). Gubernur Bali Minta Kantor MDA Diberdayakan Untuk Kemajuan Desa Adat. www.bali.antaranews.com/berita/177935/gubernur-bali-minta-kantor-mda-diberdayakan-untuk-kemajuan-desa-adat (Accessed 24 May 2020).

[79]It is a business unit belonging to the customary village carries out business activities in the real economy, services, and/or public services organized under customary law and managed with modern governance for improve the welfare and independence of customary village members. Article 1 (17) of the Regulation of Bali Provincial Governor No. 34 Year 2019 Concerning the Financial Management of Customary Villages in Bali.

Responding to the Global Pandemic: How Realistic To Collect the Contribution?

The enactment of the Provincial Regulation may temporarily lose its relevance in the following months as Bali cannot hinder the shocking impact of the global pandemic of Covid-19. Due to a massive travel warning for traveling and the restrictions for operating airport and port services to visit and leaving from Bali, tourism in Bali is now extremely reduced nearly to zero activities. The situation in April 2020 can be a strong indicator of this tourism catastrophic. There was only 327 visit of foreign tourists, some 273 through airport and 54 through the port while occupancy rates for starred hotel rooms were recorded at 3.22 percent with the average length of stay is 2.49 days.[80] It is followed by the prohibition to operate tourist objects and attraction as well as leisure and entertainment facilities.[81]

The abstention of tourist visits has caused a significant number of people in the tourism industry to lose their jobs and businesses. Considering that economic activities in Bali related directly, indirectly, and induced to tourism services that absorbing many workforces,[82] this situation is so devastating. Bali's economic growth in the first quarter of 2020 contracted by (-1.14) percent on the basis of year on year while the potential losses from leisure and MICE (meetings, incentives, conferencing, exhibitions) from February until October 2020 is estimated 344 million USD.[83] If calculated from the tourists' length of stay, the monthly loss is around 673 million USD.[84] In this situation, local leaders should realize

[80]Badan Pusat Statistik Provinsi Bali. (2020). Perkembangan Pariwisata Provinsi Bali April 2020. www.bali.bps.go.id/pressrelease/2020/06/02/717329/perkembangan-pariwisata-provinsi-bali-april-2020.html (Accessed 14 June 2020).

[81]Release of Bali Province Governor's Appeal No. 215/Gugascovid-19/VI/2020, dated 8 June 2020, point 3

[82]Antara, M & Sumarniasih, M.S. (2017). Role of Tourism in Economy of Bali and Indonesia. *Journal of Tourism and Hospitality Management 5(2),* p. 43.

[83]Tribun Bali. (2020). Agustus Pariwisata Bali Diharapkan Sudah Buka Lagi Dengan Konsep New Normal. www.bali.tribunnews.com/2020/05/23/agustus-pariwisata-bali-diharapkan-sudah-buka-lagi-dengan-konsep-new-normal?page=3 (Accessed 24 May 2020).

[84]Kompas.Com. (2020) Dampak Pandemi Covid-19 Pariwisata Bali Rugi Rp 97 Triliun Tiap Bulan. www.regional.kompas.com/read/2020/05/13/17591091/dampak-pandemi-covid-19-pariwisata-bali-rugi-rp-97-triliun-tiap-bulan (Accessed 14 June 2020)

that they cannot expect tourism to overcome all community problems and rely mainly on tourism contributions, levies, or taxes.[85]

The resilience of Bali related to the decreasing numbers of foreign tourists has proven. For the last two decades, Bali faced several occurrences including terrorist bombings, SARS pandemic, and volcano eruptions that lead to the issuance of travel advisory by many countries. After those natural and human-made disasters, facts show that Bali is always able to recover tourism gradually. But the ongoing Covid-19 pandemic is very exceptional. Micro, small, and middle-sized enterprises and other informal sectors are moving slowly. Experts raise speculations that the tourism recovery needs at least 6 months after the pandemic can be resolved, while some commentators argue that it needs years. An optimistic view comes from the national government that believes Bali will become one of the main destinations that are relatively faster to recover and visited by many tourists once the pandemic is declared over. The view was based on a fact that Bali Province has proven capable of curbing the spread of Covid-19 in the community through local wisdom and the role of customary villages.[86]

The financial capacity of Bali Province in the year 2020 is being examined. The government budgets are mainly allocated to support the basic needs of the population (mainly foods and health sectors), the continuity of educational activities, and to some extent, to stimulate business activities while private sectors are trying to survive in an uncertain situation.

The idea of supporting the natural and cultural heritage of Bali through tourists contributions then seems a little bit far from the expectation. The political talks regarding these contributions may be relevant and effectively implemented only after tourism has been recovered from the crisis. Even if international travel is opened, there is no guarantee that travel for leisure will be a priority for individuals, when the issue of health and safety is at stake.

In 2019, the Minister of Tourism issued a regulation concerning tourism crisis management (TCM). The TCM is a series of measured and systematic actions carried out in the tourism ecosystem to prepare, respond, and recover from a crisis, including a crisis caused by the health/ pandemic of infectious diseases.[87] This TCM framework consists of 4 phases: preparedness and mitigation; emergency response; recovery; and

---

[85]See Kreag, G. (2001). *The Impact of Tourism,* Minnesota Sea Grant, p. 3. http://www.seagrant.umn.edu/tourism/pdfs/ImpactsTourism.pdf

[86]Radar Bangsa. (2020). Bali Diperkirakan Jadi Destinasi Pertama yang Pulih Pasca Pandemi. www.www.radarbangsa.com/travel/24672/bali-diperkirakan-jadi-destinasi-pertama-yang-pulih-pasca-pandemi (Accessed 22 May 2020).

[87]Article 1 (2) and 4 (3)(b) of the Minister of Tourism Regulation No. 10 Year 2019 concerning Tourism Crisis Management

normalization.[88] At the provincial level, there has been an effort by the regional lawmakers to ensure the fulfillment of the standards and implementation of the tourism in Bali, in addressing the pandemic crisis. A set of rules were adopted that legitimises the issuance of policy with regards to the prevention, management of disasters or emergencies, and/or recovery of Bali cultural tourism in the aftermath of disasters or emergencies.[89]

Further, Bali Provincial Government and the Ministry of Tourism and Creative Economy have conducted a coordination meeting in the mid of May 2020, following the designation of Bali as a pilot project for the implementation of the Cleanliness, Health, and Safety (CHS) program launched by the Ministry. While there is a hope that a gradual opening of tourism destination in October 2020, it still serves as a scenario with several protocol requirements, regional readiness, and the decision of the Bali Provincial Government.[90] So far, it is planned that Bali will start welcoming domestic tourists in August and will reopen its borders to international tourists in September 2020, as long as some required conditions are fulfilled. [91]

Therefore, it is now becoming more reasonable for the Bali Provincial Government to campaigning Bali as a safe tourist destination during and after this global pandemic, instead of enforcing the contribution to tourists. A series of promotions to encourage the coming of tourists to resurrect the basic tourism industry will be the most rational choice rather than imposing contribution that may be not so convenient to the tourists in this non-friendly situation for traveling.

Conclusion

The article has revealed some facts related to the Bali Provincial Government's efforts to charge a contribution to foreigners who visit Bali.

[88]Article 6 (1) of the Minister of Tourism Regulation No. 10 Year 2019 concerning Tourism Crisis Management

[89]Bali Regional House of Representative, Final Report on Draft of Bali Provincial Regulation concerning the Standards and Implementation of Bali Cultural Tourism, 14 May 2020.

[90]Kompas. (2020) Kapan Bali akan Buka untuk Wisatawan? www.travel.kompas.com/read/2020/05/22/154200927/kapan-bali-akan-buka-untuk-wisatawan-?page=all. (Accessed 14 June 2020)

[91]Jakarta Globe. (2020). Bali Plans to Restore Tourist Confidence and Reopen Borders in September, www.jakartaglobe.id/news/bali-plans-to-restore-tourist-confidence-and-reopen-borders-in-september (Accessed 19 June 2020)

Some issues may be concluded. The imposing of levy on foreign tourist has been practiced in various ways by national governments and regions of the countries in the world. Therefore, the creation of Draft of Provincial Regulation concerning Protection of Bali's Natural Environment and Culture through Tourism Contributions ('the draft') by the Bali Provincial Government reflects an effort to make use of tourism as a means to support the sustainability of nature and culture.

The draft was responded to with high expectations in terms of offering a solution to the preservation of the natural environment and culture in Bali. Most local tourism stakeholders believe that the draft may be used as an effective and efficient means of collecting funds from foreign tourists to be further allocated to strategic sectors. In contrast, some international and local actors do not have the same common understanding on how the fund should be collected, whether through airfare tax, airport-arrival charge, or other means. They also perceived that such a levy would decrease the number of foreigners who plan to visit Bali.

The Bali Provincial Regulation No. 1 Year 2020 concerning Tourist Contributions for the Protection of the Natural Environment and Culture of Bali was then finally enacted in April 2020. It clarifies the most contending issue by determining the contributions that having a rather voluntary character, leaving the assumption that it would serve as a new type of tourism taxes, levies, or retributions. The Provincial Regulation also makes clear that the Contributions will be collected from both foreign and domestic tourists. Some remaining technical matters that are not covered in this Provincial Regulation e.g. the means of collecting and technical management of the contributions will be further regulated by implementing regulation that shall be issued at the latest October 2020.

There is no guarantee that this Provincial Regulation will solve the problem of lacking funds for supporting the natural environment and culture preservations in Bali. The voluntary character of the tourist contribution entails that the amount of money to gain depending on the generosity of the tourists. Therefore, the contributions are unpredictable and cannot be set as an income plan. In this regard, all local governments in Bali should apply minimum treatment in ensuring the tourism activities, primarily mass tourism, would not lessen the quality of the natural environment and weaken the spirit of preserving the culture and tradition. The initiative to involve the community at the lowest level, e.g customary village, in the management of tourist destinations should be continued. One hand, the local government can still collect revenue from retribution at the tourism objects and on the other hand, the customary communities as the heir of nature and culture in the tourist destination would be directly benefited from the tourism and could continue their local wisdom and tradition in preserving environment and culture.

The global pandemic of Covid-19 is a serious challenge to pursue the imposed contribution to tourists. There has been extreme economic turbulence in Bali due to the lack, or even abstention, of tourists who visit Bali, following the travel restrictions. A focus on recovering the fundament of the population's economy makes discussion and efforts to legalize the levy less important. In this situation, the Bali Provincial Government must seek to promote programs that encourage the coming of tourists to resurrect the basic tourism industry. Imposing contributions maybe not so convenient for tourists in this travel-unfriendly situation. After all the situation is recovered, the protection of nature and culture should be put again into the top list of priorities. It seems that the realization of tourism contribution as determined in this Provincial Regulation would be effective once the tourism industry runs normally.

Acknowledgment and Disclosure . The research was funded by Udayana University under a Scheme of *Penelitian Unggulan Program Studi* (PUPS) in the year 2019. The Authors express our gratefulness to heads of Research and Community Services Institution and Faculty of Law of Udayana University and the Legal Bureau of the Regional Secretariat for the Bali Province, Anak Agung Ngurah Adhi Ardana (Member of Bali Regional House of Representatives) and to all interviewees: Made Mangku Pastika, a Member (National Senator) at the Regional Representative Council, representing Bali Province; Anak Agung Komang Sapta Negara, Secretary of Culture Office Bali Province; I Gusti Ngurah Supanji and I Made Gama Sumerta, Head and Secretary of the Tabanan Regency Culture Office; Ni Ketut Mariatni Sukadewi, Head of the Tourism Destination Division of the Regional Tourism Office of Gianyar Regency; I Gede Nurjaya, Secretary of *Nayaka* (Expert team of the Customary Village Assembly (*Majelis Desa Adat*/MDA) of the Bali Province; and Ketut Ngastawa (Lawyer, Bali).

References

Antara, M & Sumarniasih, M.S. (2017). Role of Tourism in Economy of Bali and Indonesia. *Journal of Tourism and Hospitality Management 5(2).*

Cela, G. (2018). The Impact Assessment of the VAT Reduction in Tourism Sector. *European Scientific Journal, 14 (25).*

Falade Obalade, T.A. & Dubey, S. (2014). Managing Tourism as a Source of Revenue and Foreign Direct Investment Inflow in a Developing Country: The Jordanian Experience. *International Journal of Academic Research in Economics and Management Sciences, 3(3).*

Fontana, C. & Lagutin, I. (2018). Tourist Taxes in Italy and Russia. *Russian Law Journal, VI(1).*

Ihalanayake, R. (2007). *Economics of Tourism Taxation : A Study of Tourism Taxes in Australia,* A Thesis submitted in total Fulfilment of the Requirements for the Degree of Doctor of Philosophy, School of Applied Economics, Faculty of Business and Law, Victoria University, Melbourne.

Li, Y., Guo, L., Zhu, W. and Chen, F. (2010). Feasibility Analysis of Collecting Environmental Protection Tax from Tourist in an Environmental Concervation Area: A Case Study of Miyun County, in C. A. Brebbia and F. D. Pineda (Ed), *Sustainable Tourism IV.* WIT Press. Southampton.

Mahangila, D & Anderson, W. (2017). Tax Administrative Burdens in the Tourism Sector in Zanzibar: Stakeholders' Perspectives, *SAGE Open.*

OECD. (2014). *OECD Tourism Trends and Policies 2014.* OECD Publishing. Paris.

Pazienza, P. (2011). Should We Tax Tourism? Theoretical Justifications from the Economics of non-Renewable Resource Use, *Environmental Economics, 2(1).*

PricewaterhouseCoopers LLP-Europena Commission. (2017). *The Impact of Taxes on the Competitiveness of European Tourism,* Final Report. Luxembourg: Publications Office of the European Union

Salain, M.S.P.D, Isles, D. & Wairocana, I.G.N. (2017). Regulating Indigenous Culture as a Tourism Economic Resource. *Udayana Journal of Law and Culture, 1(2).*

Sedubun, V.J. (2012). Indikator Kepentingan Umum Sebagai Dasar Pembatalan Peraturan Daerah. *Jurnal Sasi, 18 (1).*

Trimurti, C. P & Utama, I.G.B.R. (2019). Confirmation of the Tourism Marketing Mix Model in the Perspective of Foreign Tourists. *The International Journal of Business Management and Technology, 3(6).*

UNWTO. (2011) *Policy and Practice for Global Tourism,* United Nations World Tourism Organization. Madrid.

Wiranatha, A.S, Pujaastawa, I.B.G., Antara, M. & Ariana, N. (2015). *Membangun Mekanisme Pendanaan Berkelanjutan Untuk Pelestarian Alam dan Budaya Bali.* Pusat Penelitian Kebudayaan dan Kepariwisataan and Conservation International Indonesia. Bali.

UNWTO. (2014). *UNWTO cautions against potential tourism tax in Africa.* Press Release No: PR14033, 13 May 2014.

Documents

Bali Regional House of Representative, Final Report on Draft of Bali Provincial Regulation concerning the Standards and Implementation of Bali Cultural Tourism, 14 May 2020.

Decision Adopted by the World Heritage Committee No. 36 COM 8B.26, At Its 36th Session (Saint-Petersburg, 2012), the Cultural Landscape of Bali Province: the Subak System as a Manifestation of the Tri Hita Karana Philosophy, Indonesia

Draft of Bali Provincial Regulation concerning Protection of Bali's Natural Environment and Culture through Tourism Contributions (2019)

ICAO. Convention on International Civil Aviation Signed at Chicago on 7 December 1944 (List of Signatories). https://www.icao.int/secretariat/legal/List%20of%20Parties/Chicago_EN.pdf
(accessed 29 December 2019)

Letter of Head of Legal Bureau of the Ministry of Home Affairs to the Head of Legal Bureau of Bali Province No. 188.341/02/NR/BHK, dated 14 January 2020.

Release of Bali Province Governor's Appeal No. 215/Gugascovid-19/VI/2020, dated 8 June 2020

Resolution adopted by the General Assembly 21 December 2001 A/RES/56/212 Global Code of Ethics for Tourism

PricewaterhouseCoopers LLP-European Commission. (2017). *The Impact of Taxes on the Competitiveness of European Tourism*, Final Report. Luxembourg: Publications Office of the European Union

Online Sources

ABC Mallorca. (2019). What is Mallorca's tourist tax? https://www.abc-mallorca.com/balearic-tourist-tax-doubles/ (accessed 31 August 2019).

Antara News. (2019). DPRD Bali Beri Saran untuk Ranperda Kontribusi Wisatawan. https://bali.antaranews.com/berita/158938/dprd-bali-beri-saran-untuk-ranperda-kontribusi-wisatawan
(accessed 29 December 2019).

Antara News. (2019). Koster: Biaya kontribusi wisatawan disatukan dengan tiket pesawat. https://bali.antaranews.com/berita/135334/koster-biaya-kontribusi-wisatawan-disatukan-dengan-tiket-pesawat (accessed 31 August 2019).

Antara News. (2019). Senator Pastika Ubah Nama Ranperda Kontribusi Wisatawan.
https://bali.antaranews.com/berita/173032/senator-pastika-ubah-nama-ranperda-kontribusi-wisatawan (Accessed 29 December 2019).

Antara News. (2020). Gubernur Bali Minta Kantor MDA Diberdayakan Untuk Kemajuan Desa Adat. https://bali.antaranews.com/berita/177935/gubernur-bali-minta-kantor-mda-diberdayakan-untuk-kemajuan-desa-adat (Accessed 24 May 2020).

Badan Pusat Statistik Provinsi Bali. (2019). Pertumbuhan Ekonomi Bali Tahun 2018. https://bali.bps.go.id/pressrelease/2019/02/06/717261/pertumbuhan-ekonomi-bali--tahun-2018.html (Accessed 29 December 2019).

Perkembangan Pariwisata Provinsi Bali April 2020. https://bali.bps.go.id/pressrelease/2020/06/02/717329/perkembangan-pariwisata-provinsi-bali-april-2020.html (Accessed 15 June 2020).

Bali Express. (2019). Dewan Bali Sahkan Ranperda Perubahan RTRW dan Kontribusi Wisatawan. https://baliexpress.jawapos.com/read/2019/08/21/151775/dewan-bali-sahkan-ranperda-perubahan-rtrw-dan-kontribusi-wisatawan (Accessed 29 December 2019).

Bali Travel News. (2018) Rencana Pungutan 10 Dolar per Wisatawan Mesti Dikemas dengan Kreatif. https://bali-travelnews.com/2018/09/25/rencana-pungutan-10-dolar-per-wisatawan-mesti-dikemas-dengan-kreatif/ (Accessed 24 May 2020).

Bali Post. (2020). Alih Fungsi Lahan Pertanian di Bali Rata-Rata 700 Hektar per Tahun. http://www.balipost.com/news/2020/01/17/99216/Alih-Fungsi-Lahan-Pertanian-di...html

(Accessed 19 January 2020).

Bali Puspa News. (2019). Perkuat UMKM, Dewan Bali Dukung Pemprov Tambah Penyertaan Modal di BPD Bali. https://www.balipuspanews.com/perkuat-umkm-dewan-bali-dukung-pemprov-tambah-penyertaan-modal-di-bpd-bali.html (Accessed 24 May 2020).

Bali Puspa News. (2019). Senator Pastika Usulkan Ubah Nama Kontribusi menjadi Donasi pada Ranperda Kontribusi Wisatawan. https://www.balipuspanews.com/senator-pastika-usulkan-ubah-nama-kontribusi-menjadi-donasi-pada-ranperda-kontribusi-wisatawan.html (accessed 29 December 2019).

Bali Travel News. (2016). Budaya Bali Alami Degradasi. http://bali-travelnews.com/2016/12/28/budaya-bali-alami-degradasi/ (Accessed 19 January 2020)

Ekonomi Bisnis. (2019). Wisman ke Bali Bakal Dikenai Pungutan US 10 Pelaku Pariwisata Protes. https://ekonomi.bisnis.com/read/20190121/12/880827/wisman-ke-bali-bakal-dikenai-pungutan-us10-pelaku-pariwisata-protes (accessed 31 August 2019).

Independent. (2019). Japan Tourist Tax Cost Levy Airport Tourism Tokyo Olympics 2020.

https://www.independent.co.uk/travel/news-and-advice/japan-tourist-tax-cost-levy-airport-tourism-tokyo-olympics-2020-a8721451.html (accessed 29 December 2019).

Jakarta Globe. (2020). Bali Plans to Restore Tourist Confidence and Reopen Borders in September, https://jakartaglobe.id/news/bali-plans-to-restore-tourist-confidence-and-reopen-borders-in-september (Accessed 19 June 2020).

Jaringan Dokumentasi dan Informasi Hukum Pemerintah Provinsi Bali. (2020). Perda No.1 Tahun 2020. https://jdih.baliprov.go.id/produk-hukum/peraturan-perundang-undangan/perda/28547 (accessed 14 June 2020).

Kompas.Com. (2020) Dampak Pandemi Covid-19 Pariwisata Bali Rugi Rp 97 Triliun Tiap Bulan. https://regional.kompas.com/read/2020/05/13/17591091/dampak-pandemi-covid-19-pariwisata-bali-rugi-rp-97-triliun-tiap-bulan (Accessed 14 June 2020).

Kompas. (2020) Kapan Bali akan Buka untuk Wisatawan? https://travel.kompas.com/read/2020/05/22/154200927/kapan-bali-akan-buka-untuk-wisatawan-?page=all. (Accessed 14 June 2020).

Kreag, G. (2001). *The Impact of Tourism*, Minnesota Sea Grant, http://www.seagrant.umn.edu/tourism/pdfs/ImpactsTourism.pdf

Mastercard. (2019). Global Destination Cities Index 2019. https://newsroom.mastercard.com/wp-content/uploads/2019/09/GDCI-Global-Report-FINAL-1.pdf (Accessed 19 January 2020).

Nusa Bali. (2018). Bali Bidik PAD Rp 1 Trilyun dari Turis. https://www.nusabali.com/berita/41956/bali-bidik-pad-rp-1-triliun-dari-turis

Nusa Bali. (2019). AP I Minta Pungutan Turis Cukup 5 Dolar. https://www.nusabali.com/berita/45662/ap-i-minta-pungutan-turis-cukup-5-dolar (accessed 31 August 2019).

Radar Bali. (2019). Biar tak Masuk Unsur Pajak Pastika Usul Kata Donasi jadi Judul Perda. https://radarbali.jawapos.com/read/2019/12/15/170322/biar-tak-masuk-unsur-pajak-pastika-usul-kata-donasi-jadi-judul-perda (Accessed 29 December 2019).

Radar Bangsa. (2020). Bali Diperkirakan Jadi Destinasi Pertama yang Pulih Pasca Pandemi. https://www.radarbangsa.com/travel/24672/bali-diperkirakan-jadi-destinasi-pertama-yang-pulih-pasca-pandemi (Accessed 22 May 2020).

The Jakarta Post. (2019). Global Airline Group IATA Objects to Planned Bali Tourist Tax. https://www.thejakartapost.com/news/2019/02/19/global-airline-group-iata-objects-to-planned-bali-tourist-tax.html (accessed 31 August 2019).

Tribun Bali. (2018). Gubernur Bali Wacanakan Biaya Kontribusi Masuk ke Bali Turis Asing Bayar 10 Dolar lokal Rp 10 ribu. https://travel.tribunnews.com/2018/11/20/gubernur-bali-wacanakan-biaya-kontribusi-masuk-ke-bali-turis-asing-bayar-10-dolar-lokal-rp-10-ribu (Accessed 17 March 2019).

Tribun Bali. (2019). DPD RI Perjuangkan 3 UU Untuk Bali: Pastika Sebut Provinsi Tak Dapat Apa-Apa Dari Pariwisata. https://bali.tribunnews.com/2019/12/07/dpd-ri-perjuangkan-3-uu-untuk-bali-pastika-sebut-provinsi-tak-dapat-apa-apa-dari-pariwisata (Accessed 29 December 2019).

Tribun Bali. (2019). Gubernur Koster Berupaya Cari Skema Baru Genjot PAD Bali.

https://bali.tribunnews.com/2019/10/31/gubernur-koster-berupaya-cari-skema-baru-genjot-pad-bali (Accessed 24 May 2020).

Tribun Bali. (2019). PHRI Optimis Wisman Tak Surut ke Bali: Rencana Retribusi 10 dolar per Wisatawan. https://bali.tribunnews.com/2019/07/16/rencana-retribusi-10-dolar-per-wisatawan-phri-optimistis-wisman-tak-surut-ke-bali (accessed 31 August 2019).

Tribun Bali. (2020). Agustus Pariwisata Bali Diharapkan Sudah Buka Lagi Dengan Konsep New Normal. https://bali.tribunnews.com/2020/05/23/agustus-pariwisata-bali-diharapkan-sudah-buka-lagi-dengan-konsep-new-normal?page=3 (Accessed 24 May 2020).

Law and Regulations

The 1945 Constitution of the Republic of Indonesia

Law of the Republic of Indonesia No. 33 Year 2004 concerning Fiscal Balance Between the National Government and Regional Government

Law of the Republic of Indonesia No. 10 Year 2009 concerning Tourism

Law of the Republic of Indonesia No. 28 Year 2009 concerning Regional Tax and Retribution

Law of the Republic of Indonesia No. 11 Year 2010 concerning Cultural Heritage

Law of the Republic of Indonesia No. 12 Year 2011 concerning Establishment of Law and Regulations

Law of the Republic of Indonesia No. 23 Year 2014 concerning Local Government

Law of the Republic of Indonesia No. 5 Year 2017 concerning the Advancement of Culture

Law of the Republic of Indonesia No. 20 Year 2019 concerning State Budget Revenues and Expenditures of the Year 2020

Regulation of the Government of Republic of Indonesia No. 28 Year 2019 concerning Type and Tarif of Non-Tax Revenue Applies for Ministry of Law and Human Rights

Regulation of the President of the Republic of Indonesia No. 28 Year 2015 concerning the Ministry of Finance

Minister of Home Affairs Regulation No.80 Year 2015 concerning The Establishment of Regional Regulations, as latest amended by Minister of Home Affairs Regulation No.120 Year 2018.

Minister of Tourism Regulation No. 10 Year 2019 concerning Tourism Crisis Management

Bali Provincial Regulation No. 2 Year 2012 concerning Culture Tourism of Bali

Bali Provincial Regulation No. 10 Year 2018 concerning Regional Budget Revenues and Expenditures *Semesta Berencana* of the Year 2019

Bali Provincial Regulation No. 7 Year 2019 concerning Amendment to Regional Regulation No. 10 Year 2016 concerning Formation and Arrangement of Regional Organization

Bali Provincial Regulation No. 11 Year 2019 concerning Regional Budget Revenues and Expenditures *Semesta Berencana* of the Year 2020

Bali Provincal Regulation No .1 Year 2020 concerning Tourist Contributions for the Protection of the Natural Environment and Culture of Bali

Regulation of Bali Province Governor No 41 Year 2013 concerning the Amendment of Regulation of Bali Province Governor No 58 Year 2012 concerning Programs of Culture Preservation and Environmental Protection

Regulation of Bali Provincial Governor No. 34 Year 2019 Concerning the Financial Management of Customary Villages in Bali

Interviewees

Negara, A.A.K.S. (Secretary of Culture Office Bali Province) Interview held in Denpasar, 15 October 2019.

Ngastawa, K. (Lawyer). Interview held in Denpasar, 14 January 2020.

Nurjaya, I G. (Secretary of *Nayaka* -Expert team of the Customary Village Assembly/*Majelis Desa Adat/*MDA of the Bali Province). Interview held in Denpasar, 16 October 2019.

Pastika, M.M. (National Senator at the Regional Representative Council, representing Bali Province). Interview held in Denpasar, 2 January 2020.

Supanji, I G.N. and Sumerta, I M.G. (Head and Secretary Tabanan Regency Culture Office). Interview held in Tabanan, 4 September 2019.

Sukadewi, N. K. M. (Head of the Tourism Destination Division of the Regional Tourism Office of Gianyar Regency). Interview held in Gianyar, 30 July 2019.

Adversarial Machine Learning: The Coming Legal Storm

Peter R. Stephenson [1]
School of Law , University of Leicester

Abstract. The intersection of technology with the law always has been slow and often fraught with confusion. Lawyers do not speak the language of technology and, conversely, technologists are uniformly ignorant of the law's twists and turns. The purpose of this paper is to bring the legal community in closer tune with the technical community without forcing the legal community to undertake an in-depth education in machine learning (ML).

A key area of confusion is jurisdiction in cyberspace. There are, essentially, two camps. One side says that cyberspace is a domain of its own without laws, governance or enforcement. The other side claims that, in most cases international law as it stands is sufficient for managing legal aspects of the Internet.

The second is correct to a point. However, there are emerging areas of technology that appear to defy that position. One of the most dangerous and difficult – both theoretically and practically – is the area of autonomous malware. This paper discusses that challenge and proposes some approaches to meeting it.

We begin with some technical definitions and explanations to frame the legal issues properly in the technical world. We then address jurisdiction in cyberspace generally followed by demonstrating a standardized way of looking at the Internet through the lens of the law. Next we present a hypothetical attack of the type envisioned. Finally, we pose some possible solutions to the problem of autonomous malware and software-driven – as opposed to human-driven - attacks.

[1]Corresponding author: pstephen@cdfs.us

Please note that this paper is focused upon United States law and the state of technology in the US. However, the author has cited an African journal article that suggests that the issues stated here are present throughout the world (see footnote 35).

Keywords. cyberspace, cyber law, jurisdiction, international law, private law, cyber definitions, autonomous malware, Internet

Introduction – the Lawyer as Data Scientist

The core of autonomous malware is artificial intelligence (AI). The core of artificial intelligence is machine learning (ML). These two concepts imply that something – malware in this case – can operate without human guidance. Granted, human guidance is present in the form of the software programs that operate the object under control, but once that software takes over, the object operates autonomously managed only by the software (software-driven).

Take, for example, the autonomous vehicle. The automobile is given sensors, software and control systems that allow it to know where it is, what is around it and what the driver's wishes are. It then goes to work to accomplish the driver's mission taking its environment into consideration and responding accordingly. The software is in control.

In this paper we are concerned with machine learning and, more specifically, adversarial machine learning (AML [2]). Before we tackle the legal issues spawned by ML and AML in cyberspace, however, we must simplify and explain the language of the intelligent machine.

The first question we must ask is, "What is ML"? Next, we need to understand what we want the machine to learn and how it learns it. Finally, we want to understand how the machine – in this case an autonomous malware, or "bot" – uses those data. Once we answer those foundational questions we can move on to the legal issues, secure in the knowledge that we understand – at least at a fundamental level – the technical ones.

There are several definitions of machine learning but they all boil down to the same thing:

> Machine learning is an application of artificial intelligence (AI) that provides systems the ability to automatically learn

[2]Lawyers in some jurisdictions typically use the acronym for Anti-Money Laundering but we use it for Adversarial Machine Learning

> and improve from experience without being explicitly programed[3].

We want our machine to learn how to identify certain things such as its environment, input data, output data and how to manage those data. In the case of an autonomous bot, for example, we might want it to learn what kind of system it is entering (banking, manfacturing, medical, etc.), what data it is supposed to locate (payment cards, medical records, trade secrets, etc.) and what it is supposed to do with those data (steal, delete, modify, etc.).

To do these tasks the bot needs to learn what the things it is seeking look like. Now things get complicated because every banking system, for example, is not set up the same way nor does it, digitally, look the same. So we have three ways our bot can learn what its target looks like.

The first way is supervised machine learning. In supervised machine lerning you provide the bot with a list of data that look like the target and tell it to go find these. Consider the old way of learning the multiplication tables: constant repetition and rote memorization. That is supervised training[4].

Unsupervised training, on the other hand, is achieved through observation. We observe and draw conclusions from what we observe. The more we observe, the more our conclusions are refined[5].

There is a third learning mode, semi-supervised learning where you start with some data as in supervised learning and deduce the rest through observation, basing your observations upon what you already know from the supervised portion. The least dangerous of these three is, arguably, unsupervised but it can be quite a bit slower than supervised since it must learn from scratch.

Another issue with machine learning is error. You will see that in a moment. We define the calculations of our bot using algorithms. This is defined as a "…set of instructions designed to perform a specific task.[6]"

Mathematically, a machine learning algorithm looks like this[7]:

---

[3]Expert System, *What is machine learning? A definition*, Expert System(2017), *available at* https://expertsystem.com/machine-learning-definition/.

[4]Unsupervised AI - AI for Complex Network Security - A Tutorial (2019). - https://mixmode.ai/blog/whitepaper-unsupervised-ai-ai-for-complex-network-security/ Accessed 20 Oct 2020

[5]ibid

[6]Per Christensson, *Algorithm Definition*(2013), *available at* https://techterms.com/definition/algorithm.

[7]Jason Brownlee, Master Machine Learning Algorithms - Discover How They Work And How To Implement Them From Scratch (Jason Brownlee. 2019).

$$Y = f(X)$$

All this means is that some dependent variable Y (the answer for which we are looking) is equal to some function f (the formula we will use) multiplied by X (the independent variable that we are given). At least that is the way that we were taught in our high school algebra classes to read the equation. The “f”, of course, was some formula that we were expected to apply to X in order to calculate Y.

In machine learning, however, things are not quite the same as they were when we were in high school. In machine learning we are given neither X or Y. We don’t even start out by knowing f. That’s where training comes in.

Our training data is in the form of randomly selected Xs and Ys that represent what we know and what we are seeking. We then do some calculations to discover what function f will give us those values.

For example, if we assume Y equals 4 and X equals 2, we immediately can see that f is equal to 2.

$$4 = 2(2)$$

If we keep f and try with Y = 6 and X = 3, we see that our f works out correctly.

$$6 = 2(3)$$

This is a greatly simplified example and in real life the Xs, Ys and f would be much more complicated. We could use supervised training to input predetermined Xs and Ys in order to figure out what f is. Then, we could see that whenever our bot sees the X it applies the f and calculates the Y.

In unsupervised training the bot is given nothing but the Xs and it must derive f and calculate Y. It is a much slower but much more comprehensive process. The process can be sped up by using semi-supervised training and that gives us a start on deriving the f.

Because, these data are complicated, there may be no f that cleanly calculates Y from a particular X as in our examples above. Thus, we must change our algorithm slightly to accommodate that possibility,

$$Y = f(X) + e$$

e being the error. This error very likely is not a single number but is more likely another formula like f. In our examples above the error is zero so we ignored the e.

This is all the data science we need to begin to move into the legal realm and consider why the approach of adversarial machine learning is such a legal dilemma.

How the Autonomous Bot Likely Will Work

There are no truly autonomous bots yet (this writing – November 2019). But there is malware that in time will be candidates for conversion or upgrading to the ability to function autonomously.

Today these bots – or botnets as they sometimes are called – use a device called a command and control server (C2 or C&C). This server issues the bots their instructions, collects whatever data the C2 requires and communicates with its hacker human, usually called a "bot herder".

The bots communicate periodically with the C2 based upon a predetermined schedule and algorithm that lets the bot find a C2 with which it can communicate. The bot herder communicates with the C2, collects stolen data and issues new instructions for the botnet.

The whole process is under the control of the bot herder and the C2 simply is an intermediary or "proxy" for the human bot herder. The goal of the autonomous bot is to eliminate the C2 and make the bot herder's instructions superfluous.

Although there are no true autonomous bots yet, there are two developments that are very close and have, in fact, generated attacks: hivenets and swarmbots[8]. Although this may seem overly technical – and, perhaps, a little silly - in fact these two developments pose both a legal challenge and a legal opportunity.

Manky describes swarmbots as, "…a scalable architecture based on integrated and autonomous swarm intelligence." This, actually, is far simpler than it sounds. Consider ants, for example. The ants work together to accomplish a task with each ant doing its particular job gaining insight and intelligence from the group – or swarm – of ants.

Star Trek fans will recall the Borg, a cybernetic collective with a "hive mind". This refers to the sharing of a common mind, much as the ants do, and making decisions as a group based upon the knowledge of the individual members. A hivenet is much the same and the swarmbots are much the same as ants.

The benefit of a hivenet is that the swarmbots can reason collectively using data collected by the individuals. The hive learns through machine

[8]Derek Manky, *The Evolving Threat Landscape - Swarmbots, Hivenets, Automation in Malware*, CSO Online(2018), *available at* https://www.csoonline.com/article/3301148/the-evolving-threat-landscape-swarmbots-hivenets-automation-in-malware.html.

learning and once trained initially – perhaps using semi-supervised training to get a head start defining the parameters of the bot master's intended mission. The swarm then can seek victims and gather its assigned data communicating with each other and, ultimately, the bot master – now the hive master - without using a C2.

Addressing Legal Challenges

From a legal perspective this poses significant challenge. For example, in what jurisdiction is the hivenet? From a technical perspective it could cover the globe, although that would be a large – but not impossible – hive. As with most cyber-related activities the most difficult issues are those involving jurisdiction.

Equally vexing, when a member of the swarm attacks a system – a banking network, for example – what forum has jurisdiction and, perhaps more importantly, over whom does the forum (of whatever location) have that jurisdiction? The member of the swarm that is attacking and exfiltrating data is under control of the hive, or, in *Star Trek* terms, "the Collective".

The easy answer – and probably a correct one, although there are significant technical challenges involved - is the hive master or the programmer of the swarm.

There is another possible answer, though, and this is the one we favor: the jurisdiction of the victim over the hacker who gave the swarm its mission.

In his draft PhD dissertation[9], Stephenson lays out a three-pronged approach for determining jurisdiction in cyberspace:

1. The Cyber Event Test, and…
2. The Modifier Test, and…
3. The Cyber Effects Test

[9]Peter Stephenson, A Framework for Determining U.S. Jurisdiction in Cyberspace (2019) University of Leicester, School of Law).

> In order to be classified as a Cyber Event, the case must adhere to both the definition of cyberspace[10] and the definition of cyber science[11] (the Cyber Event Test).

> In order to be subject to jurisdiction in cyberspace, the case must demonstrate purposeful availment within the context of cyberspace (the Modifier Test).

> In order to be subject to jurisdiction in cyberspace the case must be able to apply the standard effects test within the context of cyberspace (the Cyber Effects Test).

Of the three prongs, the Modifier Test is the most potentially troublesome because demonstrating the bot herder's purposeful availment of the victim's jurisdiction is arguable based upon a lack of specific target knowledge by the bot herder.

We begin addressing this challenge by understanding what is meant by "victim". The United States Code[12] gives us such a definition in the context of criminal law:

> The term "crime victim" means a person directly and proximately harmed as a result of the commission of a Federal offense or an offense in the District of Columbia

The key phrase in this definition for our purposes is "proximately harmed". Proximate cause is tied to foreseeability. One may reasonably ask if the defendant should have foreseeably expected the results. Applying this to the Modifier Test one might ask further if the bot herder could foreseeably expect the victim to suffer an attack from the swarm that is managed by the hive that the hacker has programmed.

This does not require that the bot herder designate the victim explicitly. If the victim fits the general definition of the hive's target (a banking network or a particular weakness in a network's perimeter as examples), the bot herder should reasonably expected that the swarm – failing pro-

[10]Cyberspace is a complex global information infrastructure that facilitates communication between technology such as computers, networks and other digital systems, both independently and on behalf of people using it. Cyberspace per se is distinct from physical space and the constraints imposed by it such as geographic boundaries (Stephenson).

[11]Cyber science is the study of phenomena caused or generated within the cyber space, which may or may not interact with phenomena caused or generated within the physical space (Stephenson).

[12]18 U.S. Code §3771 (e)(2)(A)

gramming errors, of course – could attack any target meeting the general definition, and, given enough time, conceivably would attack them all.

Technical Countermeasures and Their Implications in Law

We discussed the nature of machine learning above. Since machine learning can either be supervised or unsupervised, we now must note what technical countermeasures an adversary might use to circumvent machine learning in a system's defense mechanisms.

Technical Implications

These mechanisms focus upon learning the training set and calculating the function *f*. By calculating *f*, the adversary can determine how the defensive measures will respond to an attack and then craft an attack that circumvents those measures. This process – determining *f* and extracting the training set is called *adversarial machine learning* (AML).

The literature on AML is voluminous – nearly 1500 papers since 2014[13]. The key issues in an AML attack are gaining knowledge of the target and its defenses and deducing the classifier's algorithm. Performing this type of "learning" attack requires interaction with the target and interaction with the target implies the ability to ferret out the attacker. This, obviously, is not desirable on the part of the attacker.

Should the attacker be deduced, the three-prong test discussed in section III above would suffice for determining jurisdiction. However, thanks to botnets – and, more specifically, autonomous botnets or hives – the swarm can be programmed to perform the analysis and inject a successful attack. Such an attack is DeepFool, an "… algorithm to efficiently compute training data perturbations that fool deep networks…[14]"

While the notion of autonomous botnets – hives of swarmbots – is worrying, the ability of the swarm to derive countermeasures to an AI defense are even more troubling. The technology to analyze a defensive system, calculate *f*, deduce the classifier and create a successful adversar-

---

[13]Nicholas Carlini, *A Complete list of all (arXiv) Adversarlial Example Papers*, Nicholas Carlini(2019), *available at* https://nicholas.carlini.com/writing/2019/all-adversarial-example-papers.html.

[14]Alhussein Fawzi Seyed-Mohsen Moosavi-Dezfooli, Pascal Frossard, *DeepFool: a simple and accurate method to fool deep neural networks*, (2015).

ial training set[15] is beyond the capability of any practical single bot. But using the combined intelligence of the swarm makes such an attack feasible.

Legal Implications

Obviously, if we are dealing with a hive of swarmbots – the hive, and, thus, the bots operating autonomously - pinpointing jurisdiction is potentially very difficult. Applying our three-prong test we find:

The Cyber Event Test

This clearly is a cyber event. In fact, we may consider it a prototypical cyber event in that it occurs completely in cyberspace with virtually no human interaction (beyond the original programming and harvesting of the results of the attack, of course).

The Modifier Test

Certainly, the modifier test applies. The hive, and, arguably, elements of the swarm have purposely availed themselves of access to the target. What that availment means is relative to the type of attack and the vulnerabilities exhibited by the target. In addition to purposeful availment, minimum contacts also may be demonstrated[16].

The Cyber Effects Test

Equally, there is no question about the impact of the attack. The target is the place of the harm.

---

[15]Igino Corona Battista Biggio, Davide Maiorca, Blaine Nelson, Nedim Srndic, Pavel Laskov, Giorgio Giacinto, Fabio Roli, *Evasion Attacks against Machine Learning at Test Time*, Lecture Notes in Computer Science 387(2013).

[16]Even if only a single contact such as a probe. See McGee v. International Life Insurance Co., 355 U.S. 220, 78 S.Ct. 199, 2 L.Ed.2d 223 (1957) – nature and quality of the contact(s).

The Law V. Technology in Complicated Applications of Personal Jurisdiction

The approach to determining jurisdiction in common use in the United States is well-demonstrated in a case brought by Microsoft[17]. In this case Microsoft identified 82 command and control servers around the world and attempted to serve their system administrators.

Of course, none responded so Microsoft simply obtained a cease and desist order for each server operator. They then proceeded to take control of the servers and disable them under authority of the order. While that case has its own difficulties, it is emblematic of typical botnet cases in America today.

However, in a world of autonomous hives and swarmbots investigators and legal authorities do not have the luxury of an identifiable command and control server because there is none. However, the hive must exist at some place in cyberspace.

The primary difference between a hive/swarmbots architecture and a command and control architecture is that with a command and control architecture the bots are in communication with the C&C server which, in turn, is in communication with the bot herder. In a hive, the hive launches bots and both the bots, and the hive operate autonomously without recourse to a bot herder or bot master. While there are other, currently in use, mechanisms that do not involve AI, the direction of fully autonomous control represents the next wave of malware distribution technology simply because it *is* autonomous.

This leaves us with two vexing challenges; locating the hive and establishing jurisdiction. We will not address locating the hive because that is a challenge for technologists. For our purposes here we will assume that the hive has, in some form or manner, been located.

The swarmbots communicate and exchange data with each other and the hive, presumably, simply provides program changes to the swarm. This could be by transmitting the change to a single swarmbots which disseminates the change throughout the rest of the swarm and then destroys itself to prevent traceback to the hive.

Likewise, the operator of the hive may destroy it after placing a copy in another location. All communications are outbound to the hive and outbound from the hive to the swarm. This prevents the possibility of "capturing" a bot, reverse engineering it, and determining where the hive is. It simply does not know, unlike a C&C architecture. More important, the hive can self-learn and join with other hives. Demonstration hivenets

---

[17]Microsoft Corp. v. John Does 1-82, No. 3:13-CV-00319-GCM, 2013 WL 6119242 (W.D.N.C. Nov. 21, 2013)

with nearly 3 billion botnet communications in a single quarter have been demonstrated in 2017[18].

This leaves the knotty legal question, "Who owns the hive?" The hive likely will be located in one two places; a server owned by the operator (unlikely) or a server owned by another entity and compromised by the hive operator. As the hives self-learn and launch more swarmbots, the number of hives will increase, again, without assistance of a human operator.

Addressing the compromised server ("intermediate server") alternative, we are faced with the question of who does the victim look to for the purpose of establishing jurisdiction over the bot that compromised his (the victim's) system. Stephenson is clear that an owner of a compromised server may not be the target of a legal action but may initiate legal action against the entity that compromised his/her server[19].

This leaves us with a dead-end unless technical experts can identify the attacker of the victim server being used to house one or more hives. That certainly can pose difficult challenges if the intermediate server is not in a friendly jurisdiction.

One approach, suggested by the Microsoft case, is identification of the true owner of the hive by tracking Internet Protocol (IP) registration. An IP is the "address" of a system on the Internet and is assigned when the new system goes online. However, there are other difficulties including the use of VPNs (virtual private networks), unregistered Ips and use of either the TOR network or other, perhaps private, darknets. From a legal perspective this is fraught with problems.

The first issue to be wary of is the ability to identify the registrant of the IP address. It is typical of IP registrants that they do two things. First, they hide behind an Internet alias. Aliases are very easy to create and are extraordinarily realistic.

For example, we created an alias named Diana Schmidt with the following characteristics[20]:

---

[18]Derek Manky, Fortinet Predicts Highly Destructive and Self-learning "Swarm" Cyberattacks in 2018 (Fortinet 2017).

[19]Peter Stephenson, *International Private Law as a Model for Private Law Jurisdiction in Cyberspace*, 7 Legal Issues Journal (2019). "**Guideline 3 –** Non-consensual or unauthorized control of Internet or other network-attached devices and computers does not dictate personal jurisdiction in the forum where the devices or computers reside."

[20]Fake Name Generator, *Your Randomly Generated Identity*. Fake Name generator online tool (2019), *available at* https://www.fakenamegenerator.com/gen-random-gr-gr.php. The tool is made by Coraban Works which appears to be in San Antonio, Texas, an apparently one-person shop owned by Jacob Allred which may or may not be the owner's real name or loation.

– Nationality: German

– Address: Alter Wall XX, Lohr, Germany (with geo coordinates)

– Mother's maiden name: Pfeiffer

– Phone: (actual, though not active, with country code)

– Birthday: 31 Aug 1974

– Age: 45

– Email address: DianaSchmidt@jourXXXXXX.[com]

– Username: (given but redacted here)

– Password: (given but redacted here – both username and password work)

– Mastercard: (real pattern but not usable to make purchases)

– Full employment details

– Height, Weight and Blood Type

– UPS, Western Union and MoneyGram tracking numbers

– Vehicle details

This tool is free to use, readily available on the Internet and users may select from dozens of nationalities and countries. Once an Internet alias is created, a "handle" or nickname comes next. Typically, the actor will not use the alias' email but will establish an anonymous, encrypted email account using a free service such as ProtonMail[21]. For that account, the actor will use his or her handle. Using that account, the actor will register the IP address. That means that even if the actor is traced back through his or her handle to the alias – in this case, Diana Schmidt – the trail will end there. Service of subpoenas to the alias is likely to fail.

Additionally, these actors often use a service to mask their registration details. This is called "whois protection". Whois is the open registration database for IP addresses on the Internet. By using whois privacy the only thing an investigator sees upon conducting a domain search is the information for the privacy provider. Figure 1 shows an example[22].

[21]https://mail.protonmail.com/login

[22]name.com, *Get Advanced Security for Your Domains*, name.com(2019), *available at* https://www.name.com/whois-privacy.

Figure 1. Whois privacy as provided by name.com

The challenge from a technical perspective is clear: identifying the actual owner of a hive IP. Returning to the Microsoft case, the same challenge exists when identifying the bot herder of a current generation botnet.

Microsoft addressed the problem simply by attempting to serve the 81 domain registrants at their individual domain name service providers. All attempts, of course, were unsuccessful and the court determined that they had been constructively served.

Because personal jurisdiction can be waived, as happens often when the service is unsuccessful, the Microsoft court made the assumption of constructive service and granted the plaintiff's plea for cease and desist orders as well as the takedown of the servers.

He problem, of course, is that should one or more defendants respond to the subpoena and should those defendants not be in the jurisdiction of the forum it is questionable if personal jurisdiction would have been granted.

When dealing with hivenets, however, the issue becomes more complicated. It will be extremely difficult if not – given the then state of the art – impossible to identify the location in cyberspace where the hives reside. That is exacerbated by the hive's ability to reproduce itself without human intervention. It can be programed to reproduce, seek a new home and register itself using the obfuscation techniques (at minimum) we have discussed.

Thus, a single hive can be launched and programmed to reproduce, register and, after some predetermined instances destroy itself and let it progeny continue creating new hives and launching swarmbots. In that case there would be little or no trail and little or no way to identify the original hive operator. The likely approach – at least as we understand hives and swarms at present – would be to seek out the locations where the swarmbots deliver their booty after a successful breach of a victim.

These are technical issues, to be sure, but they inform the legal solutions available to establish personal jurisdiction over the original hive developer. Another legal challenge assumes that the original developer sells or rents hives and swarms to other actors. This is common practice today with botnets. The question then becomes, "whom does one sue?"

There is very little precedent in American law relating to this problem. Virtually all such cases in Westlaw relating to botnets are dominated by actions initiated by Microsoft. All these cases are against John Does since Microsoft developed no direct knowledge of the identities of the actors.

There are, however, a few cases that do not involve Microsoft. In these cases, the actor is known[23]. Where the actor – in these cases the bot herder or bot master – is known standard rules for determining personal jurisdiction apply. In cases such as the Microsoft "Doe" cases determining whom to serve is more problematic.

Returning to Adversarial Machine Learning and the Legal Challenge

One would expect that a target equipped with artificial intelligence/machine learning defensive tools would be safe from the impact of an attack by swarmbots. After all, the defensive measures are of a type with the adversarial measures of the swarm. In the face of adversarial machine learning, however, that may not be the case.

While we have discussed the difficulty of establishing the identity of the creator of a specific hive. We have yet to address what happens when the attack occurs and succeeds. If the attack occurs, and fails after penetration of the target, it is conceivable that investigators will be able to extract samples of the swarm bots for analysis.

[23]See, for example, 729 Fed.Appx. 112 (Mem) United States v. Gasperini, 729 F. App'x 112 (2d Cir. 2018), United States v. Hussain, No. 16-CR-00462-CRB-1, 2017 WL 4865562 (N.D. Cal. Oct. 27, 2017) and United States v. Golightley, No. 18-10097-JWB, 2019 WL 1458949 (D. Kan. Apr. 2, 2019)

If the attack succeeds, however, such samples may not exist. The swarm bot may be instructed in its programming shared with the hive(s) to deliver its purloined payload out of the victim system, obfuscate the exfiltration and destroy itself removing all evidence.

So, the operative question becomes, "how would the attack succeed in the face of ML-equipped defenses?" The answer may lie in the adversary's application of AML.

For adversarial machine learning to occur, the adversary must do several things. What those things are depends upon the adversary's chosen attack model. There are three[24]. They all need to retrain the classifier to recognize a malicious training element (a "perturbation") as non-malicious. It is the classifier's job to classify elements as malicious or not and it uses an algorithm for that purpose.

White box attacks – the attacker knows everything about the target's model and can reproduce it, making small perturbations in it to fool the classifier and retraining the victim. This is almost always likely to be an insider attack since access to the underlying algorithm and the original training set are necessary.

Gray box attacks – The attacker knows the underlying algorithm, the model topology and nothing else. The training set either must be deduced or captured in some way before the classifier my be reprogrammed to believe that introduced perturbations in the training set are real.

Black box attacks – The attacker knows nothing about the target and must derive the training set and the underlying algorithm for the classifier. The attacker does this by "querying the oracle". That consists of getting the target to respond to a large variety of attacks and collecting the results. Having done that, the attacker may be able to reproduce the training set and the classifier algorithm allowing retraining of the target.

All AML attacks fall into one of these three categories. The ability of the law to establish personal jurisdiction depends upon what data about the hive master that the technical investigative team can uncover from the residue of the attack.

The biggest legal challenge is availability of data. Without identifying data, the Microsoft approach discussed above is our best bet and, as we showed, not particularly reliable. What is needed is a closer partnership between lawyers and cyber technologists. Beyond that, a new area of cyber forensic science is necessary.

Almost no universities teach malware forensics. In a sample of the top 34 universities worldwide teaching computer science only 14 teach malware analysis, the starting point for the level of cyber forensics needed

---

[24]Mohammad Samragh Bita Darvish Rouani, Tara Javidi, Farinaz Koushanfar, *Safe Machine Learning and Defeating Adversarial Attacks*, 17 IEEE Security & Privacy 31(2019).

here[25]. While malware analysis is a very specialized field, malware forensics is even more so. Clearly, universities have yet to see the benefits of addressing such arcane knowledge. Those that do, however, are among the preeminent educational institutions teaching technology in the world.

The most difficult problem in identifying a cyber adversary is attribution. Lin emphasizes the difficulty of attribution, its many faces and approaches to solving the problem[26] by citing Rid and Buchanan[27] "… thinking about attribution is currently based on three assumptions …". Those assumptions are,

1. "attribution is a largely intractable problem because of the technical characteristics and the geography of the Internet"
2. "attribution is either possible or not possible in any given case of interest"
3. "the main challenge in attribution is *finding the evidence itself* and not in interpreting or using it" (emphasis added)

   All three assumptions, true in 2014 are equally true now. The only difference is that there now is a fourth assumption that we add here as a corollary to the third:

4. The main challenge in *finding the evidence* may be attributed to the increasing complexity of malware including botnets, swarmbots, hivenets and machine learning, including adversarial machine learning.

Thus, we have a circular problem. First, we have the technical characteristics of the Internet. Second, we have the challenge of finding the evidence. Third, we have the prickly issue of jurisdiction in cyberspace, in part due to the technical characteristics of the Internet.

Stephenson takes up the third issue – jurisdiction in cyberspace – and addresses it with the three-prong test[28]. But Rid and Buchanan's third assumption is, we submit, really the first and most difficult to overcome. It is difficult because it subsumes assumptions one and two.

---

[25]Swetha Gorugantu, Malware Analysis Skills Taught in University Courses (2018) Wright State University, The Graduate School).

[26]Attribution of Malicious Cyber Incidents. No. Aegis Series Paper No. 1607(2016).

[27]Thomas Rid and Ben Buchanan, *Attributing Cyber Attacks*, 38 Journal of Strategic Studies (2014).

[28]See Section III above

Taken together, if one can solve the challenges leading to the first three assumptions and the corollary number 4, one can manage jurisdictional conflicts in any number of standard, well-established ways.

The legal community must, therefore, address its forensic needs with the technical community so that the technical community can provide *evidence*, not, simply, data. The evidence that the legal community needs is focused upon the requirements for attribution as laid out by Lin in his Aegis Series paper (see footnote citation).

Exploring a Hypothetical

An easy way to explain the issues involved is the use of a hypothetical attack. To our knowledge, no attack such as this has yet occurred. However, it is entirely plausible, and all the technologies – if not the products - employed here currently exist.

In this attack, the victim is a bank located in San Francisco. San Francisco is in the American "Silicon Valley" and is one of the hearts of American cyber technology know-how and education.

This bank has highly developed cyber defense systems including such capabilities as artificial intelligence-based monitoring. The monitoring uses unsupervised training algorithms for its machine learning functionality. It is capable of detecting, classifying and responding to imminent threats as soon as the threats hit its perimeter. It is constantly learning from the network traffic. From the outside (Internet), anyway, it appears impenetrable.

Over a weekend the on-duty help desk engineer notices that several accounts are being accessed simultaneously and their contents exfiltrated. This amounts to a mass withdrawal of money and payment card information from all accounts – saving, checking, etc. – on the affected customers.

However, analysis of the readouts of the cyber defense systems show nothing wrong. There appears to be no attack. Clearly something is amiss however because over 500 accounts are being simultaneously emptied. There is no indication of where the attack is coming from and no indication of where the money is being exfiltrated to. The help desk engineer severs the bank's Internet connection and calls for help.

The forensic engineers respond immediately and begin to perform cyber forensic analysis on the affected servers to determine a cause. They find no evidence of malware. Whatever bot was in the system has erased its tracks and destroyed itself. Loss to the bank's 500 affected customers is over a million dollars. The attack appears to have taken less than 5 minutes to succeed and has left no trace, even within the sophisticated AI defenses.

The bank's AI defense systems are, as we pointed out, unsupervised learning systems. That means that it develops its ML training set "on the fly" and there is no preconceived training set. The benefit to that is that the unsupervised training set cannot be guessed as easily as a preconceived training set used in supervised learning. In other words, a supervised learning training set is just a database that can be stolen, modified and returned to reprogram the ML.

Conversely, an unsupervised training set notices everything that happens on the network and adds it to its database. Were it to see an effort to reprogram it, the AI would interdict the effort. The only way to do an attack is querying the oracle[29], recreating the training set empirically and attempting to replace portions of the existing training set with the modified one. Attacking the training set directly both would not work and any bot entering the network for that purpose would be intercepted.

Obviously, it develops that the only way this black box attack could have succeeded would have been querying the oracle, creating a nearly duplicate training set and imposing portions of the training set on the target. The easiest way to do that is to take the supposed training set created by querying the oracle, creating a small perturbation that would cause no damage and repeatedly hit the target with it using a large number of swarmbots. Since it causes no damage the ML decides it is OK – normal operation – and starts to ignore it.

Once the ML starts to ignore it, the attacker might introduce a bot that looks to the ML as harmless and that bot starts exfiltrating user credentials. The exfiltration might look to the ML like legitimate web site accesses. Once the bot is finished it cleans up all traces of its activity and destroys itself. There is no indication that it ever was in the bank's system and all the cyber forensics engineers in Silicon Valley cannot find its artefacts.

Now, on the weekend when the attacker is sure that the bank is on a skeleton staff it performs what security professionals refer to as a "smash-and-grab". At a predetermined time, using a preprogrammed script, swarmbots impersonating all bank customers whose credentials were stolen "log in" to their accounts. The system does not see this as an attack because proper credentials are being used and no withdrawal policies are being violated.

The accounts are emptied to remote servers that immediately ship the money to anonymous Bitcoin accounts and the servers destroy themselves and any evidence of their existence. The attack has succeeded completely thus far, cyber forensic engineers have nothing and the bank's legal team – even with the assistance of outside cyber lawyers – has no evidence to pursue.

---

[29]See Section V, Black Box Attacks

We could make this more difficult still to track if we specify that all authentication and identification of and to the servers that receive the money payloads be created using the blockchain[30]. This creates the ultimate (today) anonymity. That means that the only place where a trail might be picked up – the exfiltration – is obfuscated by the blockchain. This constitutes an almost perfect next generation attack.

We now must ask what resources the adversary would need to accomplish this attack successfully. The use of a hivenet with thousands of swarmbots would accomplish the attack nicely. The original hive is programmed to accomplish the mission of emptying a million dollars from the bank's customer accounts. The hive then creates the hivenet without human interventions and destroys itself destroying any connection to its creator. The hivenet creates the swarmbots necessary to accomplish the mission, again, without human intervention. The attack could be coordinated to run simultaneously against several banks across the globe with disastrous results.

Today there are no laws that are designed to address this. If we could gather the evidence we could, perhaps, establish jurisdiction in San Francisco. But jurisdiction over who? We don't even have enough evidence pointing to IP addresses and their supposed owners to take the Microsoft approach.

In United States law you cannot establish personal jurisdiction if you cannot serve the defendant. Microsoft assumed that the IP addresses were registered by their owners (even though the aliases made that unlikely) and served the pseudo owners.

Here we have no owners of IP addresses because the IP addresses were created using blockchain technology[31] and all communication is encrypted and via the blockchain. The attack succeeds and there is no forensic evidence for the lawyers to use. Were there such evidence the legal issues would simplify greatly.

This hypothetical illustrates the need for close collaboration between legal and cyber experts. It also illustrates the need for more and better-trained cyber lawyers and cyber experts.

---

[30]A blockchain is a database of "blocks" linked cryptographically. Only the cryptographic hash can access the contents of the block and there is no non-blockchain identification associated with it. It is used commonly by cryptocurrencies such as Bitcoin but has numerous other applications as well. – various sources including www.medium.com/@Cardanians_io/a-database-is-not-a-blockchain-7027a319311e accessed 20 Oct 2020

[31]See https://blockchain-dns.info/ with the understanding that the technology likely would be used but no service such as this one would offer the requisite anonymity.

Conclusions and Possible Solutions

For as dire as the hypothetical sounds, there are solutions. However, the solutions are not simple, and they are global. The finding of the very small number of universities globally that teach the skills needed to start a career in malware forensics is quite troubling.

An Emerging Role of Cyber-Legal Practitioner Is Needed

Further, a global recognition of what the field of cyber-legal practice requires on the technical side. The American Bar Association is typical of key legal organizations underplaying both the role of a cyber-legal practitioner and underplaying the educational requirements. It takes the position that[32], "…you do not need to major in computer science, information technology, or cybersecurity—though certainly that can help." The author does not agree.

Consider the medico-legal field. Most medico-legal practitioners have an advanced degree in both the law and medicine – usually a JD and an MD. Our position is that cyber-legal practitioners have no less need for advanced education. Certainly, a JD (if one wishes to practice) or PhD/ LLD (if one wishes only to advise) in law and a PhD in cyber science, cyber security or a related field are necessary.

This presumes that there is an actual field called cyber-legal practice. A brief survey of the Internet using Google and searching for "+cyber +legal +practice" revealed that the common definition is nothing close to the issues discussed in this paper. The focus is on cyber law and addresses the usual public and private legal issues in an Internet context.

However, like the medico-legal field, the cyber-legal field is fraught with special problems, most arising from forensic evidence in the emerging autonomous world of the Internet. Consider, for example, a defamation case in which an individual is defamed in a public forum such as Facebook or Twitter.

If the defamer is an individual who can be identified the usual findings around jurisdiction and the elements of defamation are met. The suit goes to court. However, suppose the defamer is an autonomous bot. Today we know that such bots routinely make political statements in online forums, it is no stretch at all that such bots – not even autonomous – could do likewise and defame.

[32]Leonard Wills, *How to Become a Cybersecurity Lawyer*, American Bar Association(2018), *available at* https://www.americanbar.org/groups/litigation/committees/minority-trial-lawyer/practice/2018/how-to-become-a-cybersecurity-lawyer/.

Consider some of the technologies discussed in our hypothetical. Clearly such bots – now part of a swarm with instructions from a hivenet - could do the same thing in online forums. Today's "cyber lawyer" would be helpless without outside help.

Cyber scientists, likewise, would not have the legal insights to understand what evidence would need to be discovered without legal training. The role of the cyber-legal specialist is to know both sides of the equation and help bring the defamation to a satisfactory conclusion.

Cyber Forensic Training Including Advanced Malware Analysis and Evidence Identification and Gathering Needs To Enter Education Programs

As we mentioned earlier in this paper and last year[33] Digital – or "cyber" if one prefers – forensics education is in a sad state. In 2018 our position was that even the designation "digital forensic science" was arguable as to its accuracy. That may or may not still be the case but in either case it is of less concern here than the depth of the education required to make such a discipline useful for the legal community.

The legal community depends for its success on evidence. One can testify ad nauseum but if evidence does not support those claims the case will not go well. The problem, as we have abundantly illustrated, is significantly exacerbated when the stakes are high, and the adversary takes advantage of technologies such as artificial intelligence.

The solution is a difficult one both from the perspective of willingness of universities to add courses that are not profitable – no matter how much they benefit society – and from the more important perspective of qualified instructors. The solution to this challenge truly is a "bootstrap" operation.

Lawyers and Courts Need To Become Better Acquainted With Advanced Cyber Threats

While there may be ample income in cyber law as it is seen today (which we doubt given some interviews with cyber lawyers) there are very few law firms that view cyber law as a practice in itself. We contacted several self-designated cyber lawyers in the preparation of this paper and found that they put the designation on their web sites for marketing purposes, but they really have no practice in the field. What they do have generally

[33] P. R. Stephenson, *Digital Forensic Science: An Oxymoron?*, 6 Legal Issues Journal 95(2018).

is built around child pornography, defamation and infringement of intellectual property. None of these are inherently cyber crimes even though they may have cyber elements[34], [35], [36].

We have been privileged to work with one very large law firm that had conducted an intricate cyber investigation of a complicated (at the time) breach. We were called upon to validate the results of a private security firm's investigation of the breach.

The lawyers we worked with had an excellent knowledge of the technology involved and we ended up coming to the same conclusion. Although the primary lawyer we worked with did not have a PhD in cyber science he was a prototype of the type of cyber lawyer that our society needs today.

Conclusions

There are some important conclusions to draw from this paper and the research behind it.

First, the stage on which malicious cyber event play out is changing dramatically. Although well over 80% of so-called cyber-related cases

[34]The web site "Legal Career Paths" defines cyber law as "…the area of law that regulates how people use the internet" and lists several different types including, fraud, copyright, defamation, harassment and stalking, freedom of speech, trade secrets, and contacts and employment law. It mentions nothing that resembles our hypothetical. https://legalcareerpath.com/what-is-cyber-law/ accessed 20 October 2020

[35]The American Bar Association in its "Techreport 2018" published in January of 2019 states: " Attorneys also have common law duties to protect client information and often have contractual and regulatory obligations to protect information relating to clients and other personally identifiable information, like health and financial information. These duties present a challenge to attorneys using technology because most are not technologists and often lack training and experience in security. https://www.americanbar.org/groups/law_practice/publications/techreport/ABATECHREPORT2018/2018Cybersecurity/ accessed 20 October 2020.

[36]E. F. G. Ajayl, *Challenges to enforcement of cyber-crimes laws and policy*, 6 (1) Journal of Internet and Information Systems (2016). - "Related to the above factors of poor training, remuneration and inadequate security and protection on the hazardous job for law enforcement agency officials is the dearth of experts in the prosecution of cybercrimes."

can be solved without recourse to cyber technology[37], there is an increasing number that are hard cases[38] from the cyber perspective.

For those cases that involve artificial intelligence in general and machine learning in particular, the challenges border on the extreme as our hypothetical illustrates. We are not, today, prepared legally or technically to address these new challenges. However, and much more important, lawyers and cyber subject matter experts (SMEs) are not yet prepared educationally to work together.

When the law takes on the creator of an autonomous malware system (hivenets and swarmbots, for example) it will have to depend upon expert witnesses and even then the interactions are very complicated. Our conclusion is that the better solution is to develop a cadre of cyber-legal expert practitioners who can aid the legal system in responding to the enhanced cyber threats that we see on the horizon. Perhaps even more important, though, is the obvious prediction that nation-states and sub-state actors will be among the early adopters of these malicious technologies due to their resources and global objectives. That suggests that the cyber-legal aspects of artificial intelligence need to become part of every nation's cyber governance.

We are not there yet and the clock is running out as more and more AI appears in virtually every aspect of our society, especially cyber security.

Bibliography

Expert System, *What is machine learning? A definition*, Expert System(2017), *available at* https://expertsystem.com/machine-learning-definition/.

Unsupervised AI - AI for Complex Network Security - A Tutorial (2019).

Per Christensson, *Algorithm Definition*(2013), *available at* https://techterms.com/definition/algorithm.

Jason Brownlee, Master Machine Learning Algorithms - Discover How They Work and How to Implement Them From Scratch (Jason Brownlee. 2019).

Derek Manky, *The Evolving Threat Landscape - Swarmbots, Hivenets, Automation in Malware*, CSO Online(2018), *available at* https://

[37]Research for the author's as yet unpublished law PhD dissertation on cyber jurisdiction

[38]Martin Stone, *Formalism, in* Oxford Handbook of Jurisprudence and Philosophy of Law (Jules Coleman; Scott Shapiro ed. 2004). The author distinguishes between hard cases and easy cases, easy cases being those for which a solution is obvious using well settled law

www.csoonline.com/article/3301148/the-evolving-threat-landscape-swarmbots-hivenets-automation-in-malware.html.

Peter Stephenson, A Framework for Determining U.S. Jurisdiction in Cyberspace (2019) University of Leicester, School of Law).

Nicholas Carlini, *A Complete list of all (arXiv) Adversarlial Example Papers*, Nicholas Carlini(2019), *available at* https://nicholas.carlini.com/writing/2019/all-adversarial-example-papers.html.

Alhussein Fawzi Seyed-Mohsen Moosavi-Dezfooli, Pascal Frossard, *DeepFool: a simple and accurate method to fool deep neural networks*, (2015).

Igino Corona Battista Biggio, Davide Maiorca, Blaine Nelson, Nedim Srndic, Pavel Laskov, Giorgio Giacinto, Fabio Roli, *Evasion Attacks against Machine Learning at Test Time*, Lecture Notes in Computer Science 387(2013).

Derek Manky, Fortinet Predicts Highly Destructive and Self-learning "Swarm" Cyberattacks in 2018 (Fortinet 2017).

Peter Stephenson, *International Private Law as a Model for Private Law Jurisdiction in Cyberspace*, 7 Legal Issues Journal (2019).

Fake Name Generator, *Your Randomly Generated Identity*. Fake Name generator online tool (2019), *available at* https://www.fakenamegenerator.com/gen-random-gr-gr.php.

name.com, *Get Advanced Security for Your Domains*, name.com(2019), *available at* https://www.name.com/whois-privacy.

Mohammad Samragh Bita Darvish Rouani, Tara Javidi, Farinaz Koushanfar, *Safe Machine Learning and Defeating Adversarial Attacks*, 17 IEEE Security & Privacy 31(2019).

Swetha Gorugantu, Malware Analysis Skills Taught in University Courses (2018) Wright State University, The Graduate School).

Attribution of Malicious Cyber Incidents. No. Aegis Series Paper No. 1607(2016).

Thomas Rid and Ben Buchanan, *Attributing Cyber Attacks*, 38 Journal of Strategic Studies (2014).

Leonard Wills, *How to Become a Cybersecurity Lawyer*, American Bar Association(2018), *available at* https://www.americanbar.org/groups/litigation/committees/minority-trial-lawyer/practice/2018/how-to-become-a-cybersecurity-lawyer/.

P. R. Stephenson, *Digital Forensic Science: An Oxymoron?*, 6 Legal Issues Journal 95(2018).

E. F. G. Ajayl, *Challenges to enforcement of cyber-crimes laws and policy*, 6 (1) Journal of Internet and Information Systems (2016).

Martin Stone, *Formalism, in* Oxford Handbook of Jurisprudence and Philosophy of Law (Jules Coleman; Scott Shapiro ed. 2004.

BOOK REVIEW: *Advanced Introduction to European Union Law*

Reviewed by Claudio Cipollini
Heidelberg University

Jacques Ziller. *Advanced Introduction to European Union Law*. Edward Elgar Publishing, 2020. ISBN: 978-1-78811-957-3.

Introduction

European Union law is an autonomous system of rules, principles and institutions operating within the EU Members States, and including social and economic policies focused on cooperation and human development. The EU is not merely an economic union but is also aimed at ensuring social progress and continuous improvement of the working and living conditions of its citizens.

The legal foundations of the EU are represented by Treaty on the Functioning of the European Union and the Treaty on European Union respectively, signed in Rome on 25 March 1957, and in Maastricht on 7 February 1992. In the last decades, EU law has developed significantly; the new provisions of the Treaty of Lisbon entered into force on 1 January 2009, including relevant changes to what is regarded as the hierarchy of norms and the competence of the European Parliament, as well as a move from unanimity to qualified majority for a certain number of policy areas. The Treaty of Lisbon also made the Charter of Fundamental Rights a legally binding instrument for all Member States.

Following the Treaty of Lisbon, many areas of EU law have been affected by considerable legislative activity; furthermore, in the last years the EU Courts issued important decisions in different areas of EU law such as citizenship, free movement of goods, workers, services, freedom of establishment, and human rights in general.

Given such developments, the current legal framework is characterized by an ever increasing structural complexity of EU law. The interplay between the EU legal order and national legal orders requires cooperation between Member States and the EU Institutions and an understanding of an extraordinarily complex legal system.

The book under review, *Advanced Introduction to European Union Law*, is authored by Jacques Ziller, is a concise introduction to the law of EU's institution and policy. Ziller is a Professor of European Union Law at the University of Pavia, Italy, and formerly of the European University Institute of Florence, Italy, and the Université de Paris 1 - Panthéon-Sorbonne, France. Besides the academic activities, he has also been a consultant to the European Parliament, the European Commission and the European Committee of the Regions.

Building on his extensive work, Ziller offers an insight into EU law by using essential and accessible language to the reader interested in the multiform aspects of such a complex legal field. The book addresses the functionality of EU law and policy and focuses the reader's attention on "what the EU is supposed to do, and what it may or may not do in legal terms" (page xi of the preface).

Accordingly, the book explores the sectorial policies of the EU before describing the functioning of its institutions. Furthermore, treaty provisions are subject to considerable discussion: as Ziller himself notes, "studying EU case law can only be successful if we constantly go back to the bases, that is the texts of the treaties" (page xii of the preface).

Contents and Analysis

The book contains thirteen chapters that are sectioned around three major areas of interest. The first section focuses on a set of key aspects that are fundamental to understanding the basics of EU law. The second section addresses the state of law and policy in the EU, including the rules of the Schengen Area, judicial and police cooperation, as well as commercial, foreign, security policy. The third section is an overview of the general framework of the EU and the functionality of its laws, and accounts for less researched factors such as multilingualism, power distribution and other. Each section will be discussed in turn.

The book begins with a discussion of the foundation of the European integration process (Chapter 1 – A constitution based upon international treaties). From the very start, Ziller provides evidence of the autonomy of EU law, observing that,

> …while it is an intergovernmental organisation from a technical point of view, the EU has a series of features which

> impact upon its law that have little or no equivalent in other international organizations" (p. 3).

In this context, Ziller offers an insight into the procedure for recess of a Member State with relevance to Brexit negotiations (pp., 11-13), this way attracting the reader's attention to one of the most topical issues of the last years.

The author then explains the distribution of competences and the legal bases for EU action (Chapter 2 – Scope of EU law and conferral) by using a set of concise statements able to attract the interest of the reader and make him understand basic concepts and mechanisms. Based on a practical perspective, it is clearly stated that "when envisaging an initiative for EU action, the first move of officials of the Commission, Council and EP is to check whether there is a legal basis for that action in the treaties" (page 17); this essentially means that "action envisaged must fall within a field for which competence has been conferred to the Union" (page 17). Chapter 2 also includes a fresh overview on the principles of conferral, subsidiarity, and proportionality, and on the personal and territorial scope of EU law.

Then, the analysis moves to the values of the Union and the scope of the Charter focuses on fundamental rights and EU citizenship (Chapter 3 – Values, fundamental rights and citizenship). As far as EU citizenship is concerned, the reader is able to conceptualise the legal bases of EU rights and citizenship, having in mind that "EU citizenship is indissociable from the citizenship of Member States" (p. 26).

Moving to the second main area of enquiry, Ziller captures the state of the law of the main sectorial policies of the EU, including the fundamental rules of the Schengen Area and judicial and police cooperation (Chapter 4 – The area of freedom, security and justice (AFSJ)). In this context, the author clarifies that "there are strong links between EU policies in the area of freedom, security and justice and the internal market" considering that "although the aims of AFSJ policies are focused on citizens, their development has been strongly driven by the necessities of maintaining and further developing the common economic areas" (p. 31).

Customs union, fundamental freedoms, and competition rules are the next subjects of analysis (Chapter 5 – The internal market). In this chapter, particularly interesting is the section dedicated to the external dimension of the internal market, with insights on the perspective of non-EU countries especially for what regards the adoption of a common customs tariff (pages 41-42).

Following this, Chapter 6 deals with the policy objectives of the internal market including environment, consumer protection, food safety, redistributive policies, and social policies (Chapter 6 – Policies related to the internal market).

In the reviewer's opinion, one of the most interesting parts of the book is the chapter focused on the coordination of Member States' economic and fiscal policies, including monetary and exchange rate policy (Chapter 7 – Economic and monetary union). Here, Ziller provides evidence of the strict link between the establishment of the monetary union and the need of a "fully-fledged internal market (without any limitations of free movement of goods, services and capital due to currency exchange costs)" (page 48). This chapter also includes some insightful considerations of the institutional system for monetary and exchange rate policy, as well as the complex mechanisms in coordinating the fiscal and economic policy at the EU level (pages 50-53).

The second topic area closes by drawing conclusions about commercial policy and foreign and security policy (Chapter 8 – External action).

In the third and last area of study, Ziller provides an accurate overview of the main features of EU law and the related institutional framework, including the system of judicial review. There are efforts to explain the most important features such as autonomy, direct applicability and primacy (Chapter 9 – Specific features of EU law). This chapter also takes into account multilingualism and variable geometry intended as a method of differentiated integration (pages 67-72), and covers aspects of EU law that have received little scholarly attention. In this regard, the author clarifies some issues related to the language used in the public debate, suggesting that "in political debates the motto is most often a two-speed Europe or a multi-speed Europe, whereas in legal terms concepts such as differentiated integration or enhanced cooperation are being used" (pages 69-70).

The third section (Chapters 10 – 13) continues with the description of the general framework of the EU with the functioning rules of the Parliament, the European Council, the Council, the Commission and the Court of Justice of the European Union (CJEU) (Chapter 10 – Institutional framework of the EU). In this part, the book also provides relevant information on the different powers as exercised by the EU institutions (Chapter 11 – Distribution of powers in the EU) and the system of the sources of EU law, including primary law, secondary law, and other soft law instruments (Chapter 12 – Acts of EU law and hierarchy of norms). In particular, the author dedicates some words to clarify the role of general principles of EU law in the context of the hierarchy of norms, specifying that "general principles of EU law are also used by the CJEU to interpret provisions of primary law, and therefore they are also binding to Member States in the same way as primary law" (page 102).

The final chapter (Chapter 13 – Judicial review and case law) focuses on the judicial remedies against EU institutions and Members States, as well as the referral for preliminary rulings. This part of the book offers a comprehensive overview of the judicial system within EU law, with a few sections dedicated to the judicial remedies against EU institutions and Member States, but also the features of the referral for preliminary rulings. According to Ziller, these judicial remedies are a "key element for ensuring the effectiveness of EU law" since they allow "for judicial review of any kind of EU law act of a binding nature, including on the initiative of natural or legal persons" (pages 118-119).

Based on the book contents and Ziller's analysis, the present review intends to formulate some considerations to identify the main features of this book.

Starting from the title itself, it is evident that this book has been conceived by Ziller as an "advanced introduction" to EU law. In this regard, the reader will be impressed by the capacity of the author to combine the characteristics of an introduction to a specific area of law with important insights developed across a set of chapters dealing with the most complex aspects of EU law. The outcome of such a combination is a very agile book of 120 pages that delivers a complete, yet concise account of EU law, drawing on the author's extensive knowledge and work informed by decades of academic and professional experience in the field. Therefore, this book is a real "advanced introduction" able to satisfy both the needs of students and experienced scholars who seek for a concise but comprehensive overview of such a complex area of law.

One more consideration involves the attention given by the author to the bases of EU law, that is the text of the treaties and primary law in general. This approach ensures the possibility of looking to the horizon of EU law, having in mind that the actions of EU institutions always find justification in the provisions of the international agreements concluded at the time of foundation of the EU.

The last consideration from the reviewer's point of view deals with the presence of a continuous focus on the historical perspective: in this sense, Ziller does not limit the analysis to the current state of the art of EU law, but often provides readers with a set of valuable and concise information on historical developments within different sectorial policies. The underlying rationale is, perhaps, that to study EU law, one must first understand European history of the last decades.

Conclusion

The book is an accessible advanced introduction to EU law. The concise and clear exposition addresses the title in a brilliant manner while ensuring adequate space to insights on doctrine and policy. It helps the reader through the complexity of EU law providing considerations on the historical development of the Union and the current main challenges.

In the reviewer's view, some more pages could be dedicated to the approximation of laws in the area of direct taxation and the recent process of modernization within the State aid policy of the EU Commission.

Nonetheless, there are no doubts that this book will be warmly welcomed by legal scholars and all those who seek to understand the workings of the EU. In any case, this is an accessible door to an extraordinarily complex field of law allowing practitioners, policymakers, and academics to fully understand not only the legal aspect but also the policy aspects of EU law.

Based on the conciseness and completeness of the content of each chapter, this book is also as an ideal candidate for the first approach of the undergraduate students to the understanding of EU law.

The key message arising from these pages is that EU law is always in a continuous development, in an endless tension that reflects the difficulties in finding a broad consensus between all the actors involved.

Professor Ziller's book is a fundamental compass for orientation in the EU's acquis communautaire, an unmissable item in the library for all those who seek for a concise and comprehensive overview of EU law.

BOOK REVIEW: *Private International Law: Contemporary Challenges and Continuing Relevance*

Reviewed by Janet Slate
University of Central Lancashire

Franco Ferrari and Diego P. Fernandez Arroyo, editors. *Private International Law: Contemporary Challenges and Continuing Relevance.* Edward Elgar Publishing, 2019. ISBN: 978 1 78990 689 9. 520pp.

Introduction

As the title would suggest this is a book dedicated to the role of private international law in modern times. It is made up of nine parts and eighteen chapters, thus from the outset it is clear this collection of monographs contains much material. The book is abundant in chapters, with twenty-one individual contributors from the discipline. It book aims to provide an argumentative and credible discussion of the current and future role of private international law, and it does this through the nine themes identified as separate parts, each containing two chapters, that is: Certainty versus Flexibility; Party Autonomy; Universal Values; Private International Law and Global Governance Issues; The New Challenges of extraterritoriality – containing ; Current Developments in Forum Access: Jurisdiction and *Forum Non Conveniens*; Recognition and Enforcement of Judgments; Foreign Law in Domestic Courts; and finally Private International Law in International Arbitration. This list is self-explanatory as to the range and breadth of ideas discussed in the book. Considering this, the target audience is also quite wide, and a variety of academics may be interested sections of this work, specific to their research interests. It would not seem intended nor expected that it would be read from cover to cover – rather, each section is a standalone issue;

notwithstanding that, an academic with an interest in all the parts identified may be interested to read the book in its entirety. The introduction from the authors is very comprehensive and fully explains the topics covered in the book, guiding the reader to the relevant chapters.

Chapter One - Certainty Versus Flexibility in the Conflict of Laws, Kermit Roosevelt III

This chapter begins with the theory and literature pertaining to certainty and flexibility in international law. These ideas are contrasted starting with the narrowest definition of no judicial discretion compared with the other end of the spectrum that permits judicial discretion. The discussion is then expounded concluding that more than certainty and flexibility is needed to describe a system of law because this does not tell us much. Thus, Roosevelt III continues to ask interesting questions; firstly, by distinguishing between the idea of "rules" and "approaches"; then "territoriality" versus "policy analysis" in law scholarship and finally "traditional" versus "modern" theories of law. These ideas are used to address the overall questions around certainty and flexibility in private international law. The author concludes the first section with a noteworthy observation, that a good choice of law system will have two features:

> 'First, it will deliver sensible rather than arbitrary answers to choice of law questions in individual cases'; 'Second, it will deliver those answers in an easy, uniform and predictable way, allowing parties to plan their conduct and reduc[e] costs for litigants and judges' (p. 15).

The next section delves into United States (US) history and the European approach – this is a thoughtful tour that brings in justifications for the author's arguments. The next section considers the future of the US and concludes that "certainty versus flexibility" and "rules versus standards" 'should be evaluated in terms of the degree to which they advance systemic and right answer values.' (p. 24). Roosevelt III seems to suggest that the distinction between terms is not as important as portrayed – even more so the result.

Finally, a new paradigm is offered (p. 25) proposing that good rules should be: narrow, flexible, sensitive to content, based on precedent, include escape clauses and based on theory.

Chapter Two – Certainty Versus Flexibility in the EU Choice of Law System, Francesca Ragno

This chapter continues with the same themes of certainty and flexibility, the problem is first identified in the opening paragraphs surrounding the interpretation of terms. A clear overview is asserted in the opening two paragraphs. Ragno uses many references to explain her discussion which gives it a solid underpinning, although the discussion is difficult to follow at times. Nevertheless, the depth of her discussion enables the reader to decide which literature they may consider relevant.

Legal certainty is discussed as a pillar of EU private international law, then conflicts justice is considered as a guide to the EU choice of law system. The author moves on to substantive values in the EU system before drawing a conclusion that recognises the co-existence of certainty and flexibility within the EU choice of law system. This article does answer the argument it sets out to achieve concerning the aforementioned ideas. It identifies that legal certainty has a "crucial value" but flexibility can link certainty and justice in another dimension. The research ends in asking an open question which leaves the door open for further research, this question is whether the Court of Justice of the European Union will interpret choice of law rules will affect the balance achieved at statutory level? (p. 69).

Chapter Three – Foundation, Limits and Scope of Party Autonomy, Giuditta Cordero-Moss

The title is clearly identifiable from the layout of the chapter, it is well chosen and utilised throughout the chapter. Section 1 begins the discussion with key principles relating to the concept of "autonomy", which recurs throughout the chapter and the book. The introduction postulates that the phrase "party autonomy" is a choice. The chapter draws correlations by considering the role of courts and arbitration in different settings. This assists in the overall understanding of the chapter. Relevant law concerning freedom of contract and private international law is identified and discussed.

Section 2 identifies the foundations of party autonomy and then Section 3 moves in to considering the "limits" of party autonomy which are differentiated between the role of courts and the role for arbitration in the foundation of party autonomy. Cordero-Moss mentions that courts are concerned with private international law whereas the use of arbitration in private international law is criticised for being rigid (p. 74). Furthermore, the author identifies private international law as formal and complicated, which may lead to unexpected results. The discussion covers the role of UNCITRAL and its influence within settling conflict. The next section moves to consider the limits of party autonomy, the use of conflict rules (p. 78), and history of the law using the Rome Convention (p. 79). In the context of the role of arbitration, Cordero-Moss argues that 'viewing party autonomy as a rule of private international law ensures that arbitration is run in a predictable and efficient way' (p. 80). This argument is supported with relevant data from primary and secondary sources, such as UNCITRAL Model Law, Article V New York Convention and articles previously written by Cordero-Moss.

The "scope" of party autonomy is discussed in the final section with the same rigour as previous sections of the chapter. Here the author also indicates and addresses the criticisms within the use of private international law.

Finally, the author concludes that, 'party autonomy is crucial in international contract practice. It enhances predictability, which is of fundamental importance for commercial parties. At the same time, parties may not freely agree to settings that may have an impact beyond the private regulation of their interests' (p.99). These couple of sentences essentially summarise they key ideas that are successfully argued throughout the chapter.

Chapter Four – the Scope and Limits of Party Autonomy in International Contracts: a Comparative Analysis, Symeon C. Symeonides

This chapter continues the discussion of party autonomy in private international law. It begins by stating a fundamental principle: that parties to a contract can agree in advance which state law will govern their contract (p. 101). This chapter also delves deeper into the policing of autonomy and under what circumstances autonomy can be constrained. There is a fair amount of discussion around the Hague Contracts Principles 2015 and how this legislation affects the scope of international law concerning businesses.

There are useful diagrams included within this chapter to help explain the concepts discussed. Figure 4.1 (p. 103) shows how the scope of party autonomy in relation to various systems may be narrowed and table 4.1 (p. 111) shows clearly the choice of law agreement, compared to the contract and applicable law. Symeonides also uses in parts, series of bullet points which assists the reader in pulling out key concepts from a detailed discussion.

Section two continues to identify trends relating to the scope of party autonomy, hereby developing the previous chapter. It identifies where there might be issues relating to the following: partial exemptions; exempted contractual issues; capacity; consent and contract formation; and form. The author highlights a contemporary question in relation to continued research in this area which is 'whether contracting parties should be allowed to choose a law for their non-contractual rights and duties, such as those arising from a past or future tort between them (p. 115).' The answer to this is discussed in relation to both pre and post dispute agreements through pages 115-116, the author identifying that pre contract agreements are more controversial, and as such there is a deeper discussion of these issues.

Symeonides identifies that 'the law of the forum governs matters of procedure' and that the 'link between substance and procedure is not always clear' (p. 120). These issues are developed with primary authority used to illustrate. The section moves on to consider conflicts law in relation to substance, and it discusses contractual power and contractual intent with primary authority used again for illustration, including key cases. Using this authority, the author identifies and concludes on page 124 that the conflicts of law ruled to be used is decided not by the merits of any case but by its function.

The chapter goes on to discuss non-state norms (pp. 125-8); distinguishing the scope of party autonomy form the scope of the choice of law clause (pp. 128-9) including figure 4.2 which shows how choice of law clauses may be unenforceable; and finally - which law determines the scope of party autonomy (pp. 129-30) which includes table 4.2 which highlights variations and possibilities in relation to the chosen law and result. This is an excellent summary table which brings together easily, the main argument.

The final section considers the limitations to party autonomy and addresses two questions: 'which state's public policy limitations should provide the yardstick for policing party autonomy?' and 'which precise level or threshold of public policy should be used in this policing?' (p. 131).

The author concludes with open questions which leaves the door open for further research in this area. It also allows the reader to draw their own conclusion thus far from the vast amount of information given in the chapter. The summaries used throughout each section therefore become more fruitful, as an overall conclusion is not included.

Chapter Five - Private International Law and the Question of Universal Values, Ralf Michaels

This chapter addresses two questions: 'whether private international law is "only technical" or whether it has a normative content?' and a more complex question considering notions of "universality" (p.148). The author indicates that this research builds on the ideas of Reimann considered in chapter 6. Through page 149 the author sets the scene for the article and explains key concepts to be discussed. The viewpoint of the author is clearly expressed. Next, there is a discussion around the history of universal values (p.150) and from thence a more contemporary theory is developed (pp. 152 -3). Subsequently, a series of questions are asked: 'How can private international law create compatibility between values? Does it do so through transcending values altogether? Or must such conflicts be resolved based on certain values again? And if so, where do these values come from?' (p. 154) which are developed throughout the rest of the chapter beginning with some history scene setting, notwithstanding that the author asserts that this is an incomplete discussion – hence leaving scope for further debate and commentary. There is reference to American legal realism and relevant theories, moving on to European theories- which build upon the American model. The author's overall assessment comes back to an overarching problem regarding plurality and the lack of a hierarchy. Values are distinguished into three types – substantive, conflict and meta, and two different approaches are applied and compared to these: better law approaches and higher law approaches; with some commonalities identified- the main one being that both approaches place universal substantive values on some higher level (p. 166). The author concludes by summarising the previous argument focusing on the highlighted issues. He states that 'universal substantive values have only a very limited place in private international law.' And another problem is 'plurality of values' (p. 167).

Finally, the author asks if universal values should be found or established in private international law itself- the answer is yes but not without analysis and critique, found on pages 168-173. Meta values are asserted to be absolutely intrinsic to the analysis through responsivity and technique. And this is the authors conclusion – that meta values are the only universal values in private international law.

Chapter Six – Are There Universal Values in Choice of Law Rules? Should There Be any?, Mathias Reimann

This idea behind this chapter is based upon a literature review that identifies a gap in academic discussion relating to "values." The question to be addressed is: 'Are there fundamental normative premises generally accepted in Western-style choice-of-law systems?' (p. 180). Reimann identifies immediately that "justice" and "human rights" are not universal values and discusses potential candidates. The classical model he states is in decline, which includes: equality (multilateralism); neutrality (content-blindness); uniformity (identity of results); certainty (predictability of results), (pp. 181-6). Therefore, a newer model includes values which are ascending, those are: party autonomy (facilitating private ordering); party expectations (pro-validation rules); state self-preference (enforcement of forum policies), (pp. 186-9). Thus, it is asserted that there has been a gradual shift from four traditional values to three contemporary ones. The author finishes the chapter by considering 'should there be any universal values in choice of law?' And concluding that 'choice of law rules avoid fundamentally unfair results' (p. 191) to which the author gives commentary.

Chapter Seven – Unlocking Private International Law's Potential in Global (Migration) Governance, Veronica Ruiz Abou-Nigm

This chapter considers the notion that 'private international's law engagement in global governance may unlock the discipline's further potential' (p. 196). Global governance is defined as 'a relatively open-ended and multifaceted concept' (p. 198). Governance is further explained as being "pragmatic" and unaccountable. The author indicates that they are taking a somewhat novel approach in this section of the book by using the term governance to include also non-state actors, as well as the traditional state actors. They also discuss alternatives to top-down regulation – and as such refer to the ideas as "globalization". Building upon the work of Van Loon it is claimed that any private international law theory, technique and mechanism will provide an element of 'bridging and balancing.' And it is therefore asserted that private international law 'enables communication, coordination and cooperation between legal systems' (p. 199). The research also builds upon and analyses the findings of Wai who found three sets of policy objectives- economic, political and moral. Ruiz Abou-Nigm identifies that private international law is not unconnected to governmental interests 'but rather fed by them' (p. 201), as well as other sources.

The next section considers migration governance and indicates that private international law is not meeting its full potential here, yet migration requires global governance. Again, the author builds on previous research from Van Loon concerning cooperation and identifies how it can be transferred to migration issues. Ruiz Abou-Nigm moves on to discuss how to unlock the potential of private international law for migration concerns. She does this by asking a series of questions which are discussed through pages 205- 212. The topics raised are decentralization and demystification, the latter adding to former in that decentralization due to its engagement with a diversity of actors requires inclusive processes (p. 207). The author tackles three myths surrounding these notions, they are: neutrality myth – the idea that the principle of neutrality is limiting; public/private myth – the concept of a holistic approach that transcends boundaries; and the discourse myth – the fact that rules need to be easier to understand. The author asserts that diversity must also be embraced within these topics to ensure that there is a balancing act.

An overall conclusion is proffered which brings together the chapter and offers an idea for further research in mapping out the law using the 23 objectives of the United Nations Global Compact for Migration (p. 212). The author asserts that the chapter has shown that the 'global governance debate is generating greater awareness of the potential socio-economic and political impact of private international law in a globalized society' (p. 213) and it would certainly be the case the author has achieved this objective in their commentary.

Chapter Eight – the Present and Prospective Contribution of Global Private International Law Unification to Global Legal Ordering, Hans Van Loon

This chapter begins with a strong opening stating that there are two strands of scholarly discourse: 'the inherent, 'hidden' global governance of PIL' and the shortcomings of PIL particularly 'the gross imbalances of private (economic) power in the world' (p. 214-5). The first strand is argued against and the second is explained through leading publications. The author discusses these strands and pulls out themes and attributes including similarities and differences. There is a very thorough introduction to the topic(s) to be considered. There is dialogue around the contribution of the Hague Conference and the contributions this has made to the study. This advances a further scrutiny of conventions, and it is indicated that 'global PIL unification through multilateral treaties goes beyond national PIL' in three ways: pluralism, diversity and a reflection of globally recognised human and economic rights (pp. 217-8).

The chapter moves into the area of family law, covering the Hague Children's Conventions, among others (pp. 219-221). Further topics covered in this section with reference to the Hague Conventions are legal cooperation (p. 223) and civil and commercial matters (p. 224). This research is based on and expands upon the review by Whytock (2016).

Considering global governance issues, the chapter continues with the possibilities available for private international law going forward. The potential uses asserted and analysed include facilitating access to foreign law; ensuring continuity of personal status and family relations across borders; linking PIL unification to the United Nations 2030 agenda; and migration (pp. 227- 234). The latter topic is part of a wider study and goes into more depth than the former ones, which establishes links with previous chapters on migration. The author provides useful summaries throughout rather than a single conclusion at the end, which suits the nature of the chapter in that there is a plethora of different ideas proffered and discussed.

Chapter Nine – Extraterritoriality in the Public and Private Enforcement of U.S. Regulatory Law, Hannah L. Buxbaum

As suggested by the title, this section concerns the United States of America (USA), and commences with a discussion of Supreme Court cases in the US that have 'recast the presumption against extraterritoriality' (p. 236). The author indicates that the aim of the chapter is to 'consider the current state of extraterritoriality analysis across the different modes of enforcement', particularly when 'enforcement of federal regulations varies among states' (p. 236). The focus of the discussion is on two shifts in the application of federal statutes: 'how to define the scope of a particular statute'; and 'whether and how the determination to apply local law should account for the interests of other states' (p. 237). The discussion, as identified by the heading, also turns to geography and whether this should affect enforcement of the law considering the statutory interpretation technique against extraterritoriality.

The case of *Morrison* is used to explain how Congress has only sometimes distinguished between modes of enforcement in defining the regulatory scope of a law, but it has more frequently determined the geographic scope of regulatory law (pp. 239-40). There is much more discussion as to the latter point, assumedly because it is used more often. A good selection of cases helps to explain the concept and there is a thorough identification as to the background of the rule and why. The case of *Morrison* is expounded further throughout the chapter, identifying how it caused courts to conclude 'that the geographic reach of a statute differs in private litigation and in public enforcement' (p. 243). The case of *Rico* is also discussed in relation to the decision from *Morrison*. This use of real-life examples through case law gives an honest and practical explanation of the law. It assists the reader in understanding how the law is applied and the kind of results that can be expected.

The final section of the chapter turns to a multilateral discussion addressing 'whether a state must (or should) consider the interests of other states before applying its own law to transactions or conduct with significant foreign elements' (p. 248). Public and private enforcement proceedings are contrasted, with the predominant point being the move away from foreign interest in jurisdictional analysis for private litigation (p. 250). Again, case law is used for a deeper explanation, including the key case of *Hartford Fire Insurance v California* which was the first and leading case in this area. This through examination of case-law ensures a deep analysis of the facts versus the law. Emphasising the conclusion that US regulatory laws involving foreign elements often creates conflict with the law of other countries (p. 256).

Chapter Ten - New Challenges of Extraterritoriality: Superposing Laws, Matthias Lehmann

This chapter is concerned with how law is applied beyond state borders. It explains how the simplification of extraterritoriality has led to states regulating the same person, activity or event. Which in turn lends to problems such as individuals being unaware of law(s), the judiciary facing conflict – which could also result in some countries being avoided and some markets being withdrawn (p. 258). Notwithstanding that the term "extraterritoriality" is hard to define as is the idea of "superposing laws" which is an alternative view proffered by the author. This latter term is preferred because the idea of 'sovereigns occupying geographically distinct spheres look(s) outdated' due to the overlaps between legal systems (p. 265). The chapter considers the idea that laws are in fact much wider in contemporary society and need to be embraced beyond territorial borders to ensure effectiveness, and because many variants of law are used in a global context such as: antitrust, financial, environmental, internet regulation, consumer, labour, tax, patent and constitutional law, therefore there is a wide scope of recognition. Territorial and extraterritorial are explained as simply factual descriptions rather than indicators of good and bad (p. 264), with globalization ensuring that regulation can also be part of public policy (p. 265). However, whilst globalization nor de-globalization has the upper hand- there is a sticking point between 'superposing laws and persons or entities trying to escape them by limiting their activities to the territory of a certain state' (p. 272). Lehman develops an in-depth discussion around why extraterritoriality cannot be curtailed in the wake of globalization - focusing on the failures of public international law, conflict of laws and the presumption against extraterritoriality, and how this shows a lack of legal protection when a plethora of rules applies simultaneously. Alternative modes of dealing with superposing legal systems are offered, starting at page 279 to 282. Those ideas consist of technological methods, no regulation or self-regulation and cosmopolitan jurisdiction. However, these are also not without problems- therefore the conclusion that must be made is that any method can have useful components, but none is a panacea. Designs for management of the situation are made including - promoting harmonization and unification, taking the genuine link seriously and creating conflicts rules for public policy issues (pp. 282-286). Whilst further possibilities for coping include exercising restraint in setting up new norms and accepting substituted compliance. These suggestions are not referred to as mandatory, but recommendations that would help states deal with the impact of globalization and extraterritoriality or superposing laws.

This chapter raises a lot of interesting ideas and offers a lot of possibilities for globalization and states dealing with many laws. As is indicated – there is no "perfect" solution but there are mechanisms that can be used to assist. The chapter is thorough in its examination and gives the reader a myriad of suggestions to ponder.

Chapter Eleven – European Perspectives on Human Rights Litigation, Martina Mantovani and Burkhard Hess

Mantovani and Hess open the chapter with a discussion on the variation in human rights law between Europe and the US, the latter of which is becoming more restrictive in approach whilst little change has taken place in Europe. Notwithstanding, some developments haven taken place such as domestic practices that trump EU legislation and defendants who are difficult to identify (p. 294). The chapter then addresses the doctrine of necessity and Article 6 ECHR in discussing the role of justice for human rights breaches, illustrating with examples from France and Switzerland that contextualise the idea of necessity. This is furthered by identifying how these decisions have set a precedent for other countries to follow – particularly, the court of Strasbourg is identified as having followed the decision made by the Swiss Federal Court in *Nait-Liman*. Nevertheless, the chapter does state that binding precedent has not been made (binding decisions are always difficult to establish in international law regardless). The decision at Strasbourg applied only in that particular instance – however, the court stating obiter that it would be fruitful for states to adopt similar practises, that is – an 'international custom bound to reduce the discretion granted to domestic authorities in interpreting their domestic provisions (p. 304).

The chapter continues with a profound discussion concerning victims outside of Europe and their scope for using a European court under the Brussels Ibis Regulation. The author goes into ample detail discussing potential problems and the merits of being able to rely on the Regulation.

In concluding – the problems relating to forum identification are reiterated, along with courts generally restrictive interpretations of human rights legislation. It also seems to identify further problems of cases being brought before English courts for profit only. Overall, the chapter provides a comprehensive discussion which allows the reader to identify and consider more hinderances to human rights litigation.

Chapter Twelve – Judicial Jurisdiction and Forum Access: the Search for Predictable Results, Linda J. Silberman

This chapter argues that jurisdictional developments in the US are likely to ensure a more predictable and efficient system of regulation than law emerging from Europe and Canada. It begins with some history, including the US Constitution and the case of *International Shoe v Washington* (among others), which sets the scene for the rest of the discussion. It assumes that the reader has some prior knowledge of the topic and therefore it is fairly detailed in its examination. Silberman reasserts previous findings that traditionally US jurisdiction has been more restrictive. However, she identifies that the precedent set in the case of *Goodyear Dunlop Tires v Brown* and affirmed in *Daimler AG v Bauman* has changed the outlook somewhat. Stating that – 'a corporation's affiliations with the state must be so continuous and systematic as to render it essentially "at home" in the forum state' (p. 337).

The author finds that the modern European regime matches this newly founded US rule with discussion around the impact that this case has had on jurisdiction both within the EU and America.

This discussion unambiguously leads into the next topic for consideration which is commentary around the case of *Bristol-Myers Squibb v Superior Court*. The case is explained thoroughly before its impact is assessed both domestically and more nationally within the US with reference to other related cases. This gives context to the case-law and helps to see how it may be applied in the future.

The final section of the chapter considers a less discussed and more complex notion, that is, jurisdiction and the internet. There is a very thorough examination of the key cases concerning intentional torts and defamation, which would give food for thought to readers with a specific interest in this kind of regulation. It is particularly relevant to the modern world.

In concluding, the author acknowledges that the chapter is part of a wider research for the 2020 Hague Academy general course lectures (p. 357), which may explain the detailed discussion in relation to cases and subsequent impacts and limitations.

Chapter Thirteen – New Challenges in the Recognition and Enforcement of Judgments, Ronald A. Brand

This chapter opens with the assertion that, in order to ensure the free movement of goods *et al*, there must also be the free movement of judgments (p. 360). Brand asserts that the desire to enhance trade deals, has ensured that law is created through a multilateral body, the WTO, and previously through the GATT. However, this is interesting, because the free movement of judgments are considered a part of private international law which does not have a single multilateral treaty of control, in comparison to global trade regulation which is mandated through the WTO. Therefore, this chapter identifies how judgments have been applied in the US, Europe and China. The recognition of judgments – both internally and externally – is compared, contrasted and applied between these countries. There is a comprehensive analysis, including case-law, to explain how this recognition works in practice.

Next, the Hague Judgments Project is considered, which resulted in the Hague Convention on Choice of Court Agreements in Civil and Commercial Matters in June 2005, and how this convention has led to the draft text in 2018 for a Hague Judgments Convention. This is particularly recent research and therefore brings a lot of new ideas to the table. Those researching this specific area of private international law would find this a useful starting point as the discussion goes to some depth about the proposals.

The conclusion thoughtfully brings the chapter together – and therefore could be used as a summary page for those wanting a quick read around the topic.

Chapter Fourteen – New Challenges in the Context of Recognition and Enforcement of Judgments, Andrea Bonomi

Building upon the previous themes in the book, Chapter Fourteen considers the European and national recognition systems, and the possible role of a Hague Convention on judgments. Mutual recognition and trust are highlighted as integral to the European system. This is built on by explaining how the system could be improved – by not further reducing the grounds for denial, through reinforcing the 'double convention' paradigm, extending *de iure* enforcement and by having a more uniform system of recognition of third-country judgments (pp. 395-6).

The next section identifies the role of national recognition systems and how individual countries – rather than a broader area – can develop the concept of recognition. Third countries in particular are highlighted as not necessarily having the same trust and therefore a stricter approach has been taken (p. 397). The discussion moves forward in considering ideas around trust issues - showing very practical responses to the problem stated. There is an explicit link to considering improvements in national recognition systems. These are stated as: jurisdictional filters; reciprocity and public policy. All of which are analysed, the latter gaining the most discussion, most probably because public policy is a wider concept than the other two.

The final section addresses how these issues could be dealt with through the adoption of The Hague Judgment Project. This raises new ideas and certainly emphasises the impact and role this convention could have.

Chapter Fifteen – Foreign Law in Domestic Courts: Challenges and Future Developments, Yuko Nishitani

This chapter examines the use of foreign law in various jurisdictions, how conflict of law rules is applied and how foreign law is both introduced and applied in courts. Firstly, Nishitani gives context to the analysis that takes place. There is a discussion around the designation and nature of foreign law before the treatment of foreign law in various jurisdictions is tackled. Three steps are analysed in the treatment of foreign law: 'the application of conflict of laws rules must first be determined, before the introduction of foreign law in court proceedings and the ways to ascertain foreign law can be discussed' (p. 419). Next, the author confronts the challenges posed in a contemporary world, namely a lack of harmonization. Solutions to this problem are ascertained including the mandatory or facultative application of conflicts rules, improving access to foreign law, administrative cooperation and judicial cooperation. The author brings these ideas together before concluding.

This is a very factual and informative chapter relating to jurisdiction and how problems can be addressed. Written concisely, it is an excellent read for readers who are relatively new to this subject matter.

Chapter Sixteen – the Challenge of Accommodating Foreign Law in Domestic Courts, Louise Ellen Teitz

This chapter Teitsz's research on weaknesses in the approaches taken by courts when considering foreign law and the subsequent impact on the development of law. Teitz uses a sample of federal and state cases to assess whether any changes have since taken place. The following trends are identified: First, that foreign law in the US has increasingly not only refereed to other states but also other countries. Second, the proliferation of amicus curiae briefs is identified. Third, the growing amount of time federal courts spend obtaining the content of foreign or international law. It is also stated that this does not apply solely to the US. Two key failures of US courts in applying foreign law are highlighted – 1) ascertaining the content of any actual foreign law; and 2) applying that foreign law both in the choice of law analysis and, if selected, as the applicable law (p. 440). Animal science and the case of *Animal Science Products, Inc. v. Hebei Welcome Pharmaceutical Co.*, are used to give context to the ideas mentioned above. This is a useful section in showing the real practicalities of decisions, and how foreign law content must be found when there is an increasing use of foreign law in US cases. The discussion moves to consider how rules have been introduced to prohibit the use of foreign law in court decisions. Again, examples are used and relevant commentary from recognised speakers. This shows clearly both sides of the picture and how the use of foreign law has and has not been applied.

The next section addresses whether courts still take a laissez-faire attitude towards using foreign law if it is not instigated through the parties. Rule 44.1 of the Federal Rules of Civil Procedure is considered along with Advisory Committee Notes and relevant case law.

Finally, cross-border models are considered encompassing: amicus; certification; enhanced judicial/administrative cooperation; direct judicial communication; and clearinghouses and networks. This gives a thorough overview of mechanisms that can be used for cooperation.

Chapter Seventeen – Private International Law in International Arbitration, George A. Bermann

This chapter begins with a brief explanation of the role of private international law, which to a novice would be particularly useful, perhaps more so at the beginning of the book than the penultimate chapter. This section is devoted to the additional level of complexity arbitration brings to private international law matters, both within courts and tribunals. Firstly, arbitration in national courts is discussed identifying three points that: there has been an acceleration of international arbitration; a lack of autonomy; and the applicable law. Judicial jurisdiction is identified using case-law to give context to the situation. This leads clearly into the next mini topic of choice of law in national court, and then the recognition and enforcement of awards. The structure here is very clear and develops a story that the reader can follow.

The chapter shifts to the consideration of arbitral forums, firstly identifying how arbitral jurisdiction is different to that of judicial. This creates an interesting distinction. The discussion develops as above, in that case law is used for explanation and then mini topics of choice of law in an arbitral form is discussed followed by the recognition and enforcement of awards. This allows a pattern to emerge and thus shows clearly the distinction between awards made judicially or through arbitration.

Chapter Eighteen – Private International Law and Arbitration: Arbitral Determination of the Law or Rules of Law Governing the Merits, Horacio A. Grigera Naon

In this final chapter, the notion of arbitration is continued. It is identified clearly as a separate mode of justice to the "private" nature of it – it is not part of the judiciary. But that does not mean that decisions are taken by "free-will"; there are parameters that arbitrators will abide by. Notwithstanding that, disputes are decided on a case-by-case basis without precedent but guided by "reasonableness". These issues are addressed in this final, short, chapter. If one is looking for an in-depth discussion of arbitration, this chapter will not suffice, but it does create interesting discussions. The term reasonable is analysed, with identification as to how this concept can be used in practice. Reference to the International Chamber of Commerce rules is made to give an illustrative example. This is useful to see the realistic application of a set of rules to a given dispute. Finally, illustrative examples of ICC arbitration awards are given.

Conclusion

Overall, this book most certainly addresses a myriad of issues in relation to private international law. It is a very thorough all round text, abundant of detail and analysis. It does, however, require some prior understanding of the concept of private international law and is therefore not for the novice.

The level of detail lends to excellent and thought-provoking discussions. It also leaves open questions for further research and study.

The chapters are organised such that each section can be read as standalone issue (i.e. each mini section of two chapters) and chapters are independent of others, making it possible to read them in any given order. However, chapters in each section are linked thematically, and therefore it would be wise to consider them together.

www.ingramcontent.com/pod-product-compliance
Lightning Source LLC
LaVergne TN
LVHW022101200926
848481LV00003B/1024
* 9 7 9 8 2 1 5 3 9 6 7 5 9 *